The People's Bible Teachings

HEAVEN AND HELL

Eternal Life, Eternal Punishment

Brian R. Keller

NORTHWESTERN PUBLISHING HOUSE
Milwaukee, Wisconsin

Library of Congress Control Number: 2006921501
Northwestern Publishing House
1250 N. 113th St., Milwaukee, WI 53226-3284
www.nph.net
© 2007 by Northwestern Publishing House
Published 2007
Printed in the United States of America
ISBN 978-0-8100-1978-2
ISBN 978-0-8100-2608-7 (e-book)

22 23 24 25 26 27 28 29 30   14 13 12 11 10 9 8 7 6

Table of Contents

Editor's Preface

The People's Bible Teachings is a series of books on all of the main doctrinal teachings of the Bible.

Following the pattern set by The People's Bible series, these books are written especially for laypeople. Theological terms, when used, are explained in everyday language so that people can understand them. The authors show how Christian doctrine is drawn directly from clear passages of Scripture and then how those doctrines apply to people's faith and life. Most importantly, these books show how every teaching of Scripture points to Christ, our only Savior.

The authors of The People's Bible Teachings are parish pastors and professors who have had years of experience teaching the Bible. They are men of scholarship and practical insight.

We take this opportunity to express our gratitude to Professor Leroy Dobberstein of Wisconsin Lutheran Seminary, Mequon, Wisconsin, and Professor Thomas Nass of Martin Luther College, New Ulm, Minnesota, for serving as consultants for this series. Their insights and assistance have been invaluable.

We pray that the Lord will use these volumes to help his people grow in their faith, knowledge, and understanding of his saving teachings, which he has revealed to us in the Bible. To God alone be the glory.

Curtis A. Jahn
Series Editor

Introduction

Death is not the most pleasant topic to discuss. Many people are afraid of dying. They fear the unknown. They fear the judgment of God. Yet, deep down, they know it's coming. There is a saying: The only sure things are death and taxes. Actually, you might elude taxes, but not death.

What happens at death? The question is quite broad, requiring answers at many levels. God knows all the answers, but he has not revealed everything. He has revealed everything we need to know, however. "The secret things belong to the LORD our God, but the things revealed belong to us and to our children forever" (Deuteronomy 29:29). We can be certain of the answers God has revealed in Scripture. Whatever the Bible teaches about death is absolutely true.

Some of us may have some experience with death. Maybe we've been at the bedsides of friends or relatives who have died. One minute we were talking with them, and then they were gone. We don't see what they experience next. We can see a lifeless body and the reaction. There might be a frantic attempt to resuscitate the person. There might be great sorrow or peace and quiet. There might be a mixed reaction, as believers struggle with the sorrow of separation from this loved one and yet enjoy by faith the assurance that this person's soul rests safely and comfortably with Jesus.

What happens when you are dying? What is it like to face a long struggle with a terminal illness? You might be afraid. You might deny that it is happening. You might become angry or depressed. You might finally accept the fact that you are dying. But still you might wonder: What is it like to die suddenly and unexpectedly, as in a violent accident or in peaceful slumber? What is it like to die? What is it like in the very moment of death?

Can we really know what it is like to die before we experience it? One cardiologist with plenty of experience in resuscitating patients wrote, "Contrary to what most people think, it doesn't hurt!" When his patients' hearts stopped, he regarded them as clinically dead. Sometimes, after cardiopulmonary resuscitation (CPR), their hearts started again. The doctor observed:

> Strangely, people who have died do not seem to fear the moment of death again. And yet patients who have not experienced death seem to fear death the most, although none of them seem to express a fear of judgment—the one thing feared most by those who have actually been beyond death's door![1]

We cannot be certain that this doctor is right about the moment of death in every case. But we can agree with his general assessment that people should be more concerned about God's judgment. Hebrews 9:27 says, "Man is destined to die once, and after that to face judgment." That judgment will remain in effect for all eternity. It will mean "eternal life" or "eternal punishment" (Matthew 25:46).

People who believe in Jesus as their Savior from sin do not need to fear death. We can be sure that Jesus, our Savior and Good Shepherd, will be with us all the way. We can join David in saying, "Even though I walk through the valley of the shadow of death, I will fear no evil, for you are with me" (Psalm 23:4).

For believers, death is only a sleep. Before Jesus raised the daughter of Jairus, he said, "Why all this commotion and wailing? The child is not dead but asleep" (Mark 5:39). Jesus said the same about another believer he was about to raise from death. "Our friend Lazarus has fallen asleep; but I am going there to wake him up" (John 11:11). Scripture speaks the same way of King David. "When David had served God's purpose in his own generation, he fell asleep; he was buried with his fathers and his body decayed" (Acts 13:36). Death is only a sleep because we will be raised from death. The inspired apostle Paul wrote:

> Brothers, we do not want you to be ignorant about those who fall asleep, or to grieve like the rest of men, who have no hope. We believe that Jesus died and rose again and so we believe that God will bring with Jesus those who have fallen asleep in him. According to the Lord's own word, we tell you that we who are still alive, who are left till the coming of the Lord, will certainly not precede those who have fallen asleep. (1 Thessalonians 4:13-15)

Let us search the Scriptures to learn what God has revealed to us about death, judgment, and the only two possible destinations after death: heaven and hell. Jesus describes heaven and hell and summarizes his final judgment when he says in Matthew 25:46, "Then they [the unbelievers] will go away to eternal punishment, but the righteous [the believers] to eternal life." Hell is *eternal punishment*. Heaven is *eternal life*. *Eternal* means "forever." This should get the attention of everyone. When our time here on earth is done, each of us will spend eternity in heaven or in hell.

Though we deserve the eternal punishment of hell because of our sins, God has opened the door to eternal life in Jesus. "For God so loved the world that he gave his

one and only Son, that whoever believes in him shall not
perish but have eternal life" (John 3:16).

May God bless your study of his Word.

1

Death Defined

We are not born with a clear knowledge of death. The most natural assumption is that we will just keep living. A lifetime of experience does not provide much information about death either. But we do have reliable answers to many questions we might have about death. God reveals all that we need to know about death in his Word, the Bible. Let us search the Scriptures to better understand what death is and why people die.

What is the origin of death?

If death doesn't seem natural, there is a good reason for that. God did not design Adam and Eve to die. God created Adam and Eve to be perfect and without sin. God gave them life. They had no reason to expect death as long as they remained perfect and sinless.

In the Garden of Eden, God gave our first parents a wonderful, perfect place to live. God gave them plenty of food and drink. God gave them many great blessings, including loving companionship with each other and perfect fellowship with him. God gave them an opportunity to praise and worship him by obeying his one command. The Lord said, "You are free to eat from any tree in the garden; but you must not eat from the tree of the knowledge of good and evil, for when you eat of it you will surely die" (Genesis 2:16,17). The command was clear, and so was the punishment. Disobeying God's command would be a sin. Sin would bring death.

The rest is Bible history. Satan used a serpent to tempt Eve and then Adam to disobey God's command. They disobeyed God and fell into sin. Many terrible consequences followed. God said to the man, "By the sweat of your brow you will eat your food until you return to the ground, since from it you were taken; for dust you are and to dust you will return" (Genesis 3:19). In other words, Adam and Eve would die. They would return to dust. Sin brought death.

First, sin brought *spiritual death*, as Adam and Eve found themselves separated for a time from the perfect comfort and joy of fellowship with their loving, holy Creator. They felt guilt and fear and hid from God when he came to them seeking repentance. Later, Adam and Eve would experience *physical death* too. But long before that happened, God called them to repentance. He did not want his precious creations to experience *eternal death*. So God promised a Savior from sin, who would bring salvation and eternal life. The Lord said, "I will put enmity between you [Satan] and the woman, and between your offspring and hers; he will crush your head, and you will strike his heel" (Genesis 3:15). That promised Savior would place enmity, active hatred, between believers and the devil by bringing people back to God. He would crush the head of the devil. He would overcome Satan's power and wicked plans. But the Savior would suffer pain in the process. The "he" and "his" mentioned in Genesis 3:15 is Jesus. God's promise was fulfilled when Jesus died on the cross and won forgiveness for all of our sins.

Who dies?

We are all subject to *physical death*. Romans 5:12 explains, "Sin entered the world through one man, and death through sin, and in this way death came to all men, because all sinned." Adam and Eve passed sin on to their descendants. Since we are all descendants of Adam and Eve, we all have inherited sin. Sin brings consequences. Among these consequences is death: "For the wages of sin is death" (Romans 6:23).

So Adam and Eve died. Their descendants died too. It is sad to read these words of Scripture, "Altogether, Adam lived 930 years, and then he died. . . . Seth lived 912 years, and then he died. . . . Enosh lived 905 years, and then he died" (Genesis 5:5-11). The refrain continues, "and then he died . . . and then he died. . . ." And so it has continued to this very day. If the world doesn't end soon enough, you and I will die too.

What happens at death?

Ecclesiastes 12:7 delivers a clear, concise answer to the question of what happens at death. "The dust returns to

the ground it came from, and the spirit returns to God
who gave it." The *dust* in this passage refers to the body.
At death, the dust (the physical body) returns to the
ground. God explained this after the fall into sin. "By the
sweat of your brow you will eat your food until you return
to the ground, since from it you were taken; for dust you
are and to dust you will return" (Genesis 3:19). Psalm 90:3
praises God for having the power and right to decide when
we will die. "You turn men back to dust, saying, 'Return to
dust, O sons of men.'"

Even before the body begins to show signs of decaying
and returning to dust, "the spirit [or soul] returns to God
who gave it" (Ecclesiastes 12:5). A person dies when the
soul separates from the body. We call this *physical death*.
Physical death is *the separation of the soul from the body*.

What is a soul?

It can be difficult to try to explain and define what a
soul is. A careful study of many Bible passages reveals
that the soul is an invisible part of us which God created.
The soul is the counterpart to the body. When we are
physically alive, we are composed of a body and a soul.
We can see the body, but we can't see the soul. The soul
gives the body life. It is the center of our thinking (intel-
lect), our desires (will), and our feelings (emotions). We
will learn more about the soul as we study death. The
soul does not die; it is immortal. When you die, you are
your soul. You depart from your body. So we might say
that your soul is your life, whether in the body or out of
the body (after death).

Physical death is also called *temporal death* because it is
the separation of the soul from the temporal blessings of
God. When we die, we (our souls) leave this world

behind. We leave our bodies and all of our possessions. Sometimes, people find this out too late.

Our Savior told a parable about a rich man who was blessed with a great harvest. He thought he could keep all of this for himself. He thought he would have it for many years. "But God said to him, 'You fool! This very night your life [Greek: soul] will be demanded from you. Then who will get what you have prepared for yourself?'" (Luke 12:20). God demanded his soul from him. This meant that he had to die on that very night. When his soul left his body, he would be dead. The point of Jesus' parable flowed from the certain knowledge that when the rich man died, he would have to leave all of his possessions behind. This makes many people afraid of death. Death separates us from many things that are familiar in this world. It separates us from God's temporal blessings, the blessings we see in this lifetime.

Believers do not need to be afraid of death. They can even look forward to dying. The inspired apostle Paul wrote in 2 Corinthians 5:8, "We are confident, I say, and would prefer to be away from the body and at home with the Lord." Believers can be confident, and even prefer, to be away from the body. We are away from the body when our souls separate from our bodies at death. We believers prefer that because then we will be at home with the Lord. We (our souls) will be with him in heaven.

So, as a summary, James 2:26 says, "The body without the spirit is dead." A body without a soul is dead. The Bible defines physical (temporal) death as the separation of the soul from the body. This is not a permanent condition. It lasts only until the resurrection of the body on the Last Day. On that day, judgment day, body and soul will be reunited.

Is death the end of the soul?

When we think of death, we might think of a dead body in a casket. As explained in James 2:26, "The body without the spirit is dead." But what about the soul? Is the soul dead too? No, the soul does not die at all. It lives on. Jesus says in Matthew 10:28, "Do not be afraid of those who kill the body but cannot kill the soul. Rather, be afraid of the One who can destroy both soul and body in hell." People can kill the body. Wicked people sometimes do terrible things to the body. The body is mortal. It is subject to decay at death. But people cannot kill the soul. The soul is immortal, so we believers should not be afraid of people who would persecute us. They might be able to do terrible things to our bodies, but our souls will live eternally in heaven. If we are going to fear anyone, we should fear God, who can destroy both soul and body in hell. That destruction is "everlasting destruction" (2 Thessalonians 1:9). It never ends. The soul does not go out of existence.

The soul is very precious and very valuable because it lives on forever after this life is over. Jesus asked this searching question: "What good is it for a man to gain the whole world, yet forfeit his soul?" (Mark 8:36). As the rich man in our Savior's parable found out, you can't take earthly riches with you when you die. It is more important to be sure that your soul is going to heaven for all eternity than to become rich here on earth. To forfeit your soul means to be condemned to hell.

In the first century, believers were persecuted. Some died terrible deaths as martyrs. It might have seemed that Christianity was a losing cause. But the apostle John received an amazing vision from the Lord. He wrote, "I saw the souls of those who had been beheaded because of their testimony for Jesus and because of the word of God"

(Revelation 20:4). He saw the souls of the martyrs in heaven! Souls do not die, they live on forever.

Is death the end of the body?

The body, as anyone knows, is subject to death and decay. We don't have to talk about what specifically happens in the grave. The body is slowly reduced to dust and ashes. That might look like the end of the body, but it isn't. Jesus says, "A time is coming when all who are in their graves will hear his voice and come out—those who have done good will rise to live, and those who have done evil will rise to be condemned" (John 5:28,29). There will be a resurrection of the body on the Last Day. Jesus will raise all the dead. Believers are those who have done good. They will live forever in heaven with body and soul. Unbelievers are those who have done evil. They will be condemned to hell, to spend eternity there, body and soul.

Old Testament believers knew that the dead would rise. Daniel 12:2 says, "Multitudes who sleep in the dust of the earth will awake: some to everlasting life, others to shame and everlasting contempt." Even in the Old Testament, the Lord described death as a sleep because the bodies of the dead will awaken to life again. Believers will go to everlasting life. Unbelievers will go to shame and everlasting contempt. Old Testament believers looked forward to the resurrection. Here's what one wrote: "I know that my Redeemer lives, and that in the end he will stand upon the earth. And after my skin has been destroyed, yet in my flesh I will see God; I myself will see him with my own eyes—I, and not another. How my heart yearns within me!" (Job 19:25-27).

This thought brought Job comfort in the midst of his suffering. He knew that at the end, his Savior would stand on the earth. Job knew that long after he had died, after his skin had decayed, he would rise again. He would see God with his own eyes, in his own glorified body (flesh). He longed for that day. What faith God had given to Job, which enabled him to say this in spite of all his pain and agony!

What is spiritual death?

Usually, when we talk about dying, we mean physical death, when the soul separates from the body. But there is *spiritual death* too. This is what Adam and Eve experienced on the very day that they sinned. They felt a spiritual separation from God, so that they wanted to hide. The Lutheran theologian Dr. Siegbert Becker explained a common misconception about death:

> Because men are so prone to identify death with non-existence, with unconsciousness, it is well to point out that this is a mistake. According to Scripture Adam died on the day he ate of the forbidden fruit. Terrified and hiding in the bushes of the garden he was separated from all the spiritual blessings that had been his in that joyful communion with God in which he was created.[2]

Adam and Eve passed spiritual death down to their descendants too. The apostle Paul wrote, "As for you, you were dead in your transgressions and sins. But because of his great love for us, God, who is rich in mercy, made us alive with Christ even when we were dead in transgressions—it is by grace you have been saved (Ephesians 2:1,4,5). We were born dead in sin. We were born on the wrong side of God. But God gave us life in Christ. He brought us to faith in our Savior. Colossians 2:13 explains, "When you were dead in your sins . . . God made you alive with Christ." Notice that God did all the work of saving us and bringing us to faith in Jesus. We were dead.

So, spiritual death is *the separation of the unbeliever from God's spiritual blessings*. Unbelievers are spiritually dead. We came into this world spiritually dead. If someone remains spiritually dead, eventually physical death moves that person into another category of death.

What is eternal death?

People who die in unbelief are not only spiritually dead and physically dead, they also enter *eternal death*. Eternal death is *the separation of the unbeliever from God's eternal blessings*. Jesus will be the judge on judgment day. He will say to all unbelievers on that day, "Depart from me, you who are cursed, into the eternal fire prepared for the devil and his angels" (Matthew 25:41). They will not go to heaven. They will not enjoy God's eternal grace and blessing. They will never know God's favor. They will be separated from his good grace forever.

Jesus made this point more than once. He says in Matthew 8:12, "The subjects of the kingdom will be thrown outside, into the darkness, where there will be weeping and gnashing of teeth." He stresses the separation from the gracious presence of God with the words "thrown outside." In the account of the rich man and poor Lazarus, we learn of a great divide, "a great chasm" between heaven and hell, "so that those who want to go from here to you cannot, nor can anyone cross over from there to us" (Luke 16:26).

In the book of Revelation, we hear of a second death, which is eternal death. "Then death and Hades were thrown into the lake of fire. The lake of fire is the second death" (20:14). The next chapter describes the unbelievers who are condemned to eternal death. "The cowardly, the unbelieving, the vile, the murderers, the sexually immoral, those who practice magic arts, the idolaters and all liars—their place will be in the fiery lake of burning sulfur. This is the second death" (21:8). This second death is not the end of existence, as we will see. It is everlasting punishment.

So, eternal death is separation from God's eternal blessings for all eternity. God will finally condemn all unbelievers to eternal punishment in hell, where they will always be separated from God's grace and blessing.

Death = Separation	
physical death	the separation of the soul from the body
spiritual death	the separation of the unbeliever from God's spiritual blessings
eternal death	the separation of the unbeliever from God's eternal blessings

What is our time of grace?

We have only one chance to avoid being condemned to hell. We are born on the road to hell. If left to ourselves, we would only continue on this road to hell. This life is our only opportunity to hear the good news of Jesus, to be brought to faith by the Holy Spirit's power, and to be saved from everlasting condemnation for our sins. Since this life is our only chance, we call it our *time of grace*.

Our time of grace ends at our physical death or on judgment day, whichever comes first. Hebrews 9:27 states very plainly, "Man is destined to die once, and after that to face judgment." And that's it. This life is our only chance to hear the gospel and believe. After that, it will be too late. So the apostle pleads, saying, "I tell you, now is the time of God's favor, now is the day of salvation" (2 Corinthians 6:2). The following hymn stanza reflects the urgency in God's gospel invitation:

> Delay not! Delay not, O sinner, to come,
> For mercy still lingers and calls you today.
> Its voice is not heard in the vale of the tomb;
> Its message, unheeded, will soon pass away.
> (*Christian Worship* [CW] 337:2)

This life is our only chance to tell our children or grandchildren about Jesus. It is our only opportunity to do mission work. May we make the most of it! In fact, this is the very reason judgment day has not yet arrived. Jesus says, "This gospel of the kingdom will be preached in the whole world as a testimony to all nations, and then the end will come" (Matthew 24:14). There is a reason why that Last Day seems delayed. "The Lord is not slow in keeping his promise, as some understand slowness. He is patient with you, not wanting anyone to perish, but everyone to come to repentance" (2 Peter 3:9).

How do believers view death?

While death is not a pleasant thought, we have nothing to fear from it. Jesus has gone before us. He finished the work of paying for our sins on the cross and then "gave up his spirit" (John 19:30). He really died. His soul separated from his body and went to be with his heavenly Father until Easter Sunday. When Jesus rose from the dead, his soul and body were reunited. Jesus' death has fully atoned for our sins. His resurrection assures us that he satisfied God's justice and won forgiveness for all of us. Through faith in him, we will go to heaven.

We don't need to be afraid to die. When Stephen died as a martyr, he confidently prayed, "Lord Jesus, receive my spirit" (Acts 7:59). Paul even looked forward to dying, and wrote, "I desire to depart and be with Christ, which is better by far" (Philippians 1:23). It is better by far to depart from this life and be with Jesus in heaven. The apostle Paul was inspired to write about this in another place. "We are confident, I say, and would prefer to be away from the body and at home with the Lord" (2 Corinthians 5:8). Believers sing:

> For me to live is Jesus;
> To die is gain for me.
> So, when my Savior pleases,
> I meet death willingly. (CW 606:1)

2

Only Two Destinations after This Life: Heaven and Hell

What does your soul look like? Does it look like a ghost in the shape of your body? The simple answer is that it doesn't look like anything. Your soul is invisible. We can't see it any more than we can see angels protecting us.

Nevertheless, in a special vision, the apostle John "saw the souls of those who had been beheaded because of their testimony for Jesus and because of the word of God" (Revelation 20:4). Somehow, God made it possible for the apostle John to see the souls of martyrs in heaven. In that heavenly vision, the souls of these martyrs were not only visible to John but recognizable too. They must have looked like the people who died.

Angels seem comparable to our souls in this one respect: they are invisible too. All angels are "ministering spirits sent to serve those who will inherit salvation" (Hebrews 1:14). Since they are invisible spirits, we can't see the holy angels serving us and protecting us.

But the Bible reveals that sometimes people were able to see angels. The Lord permitted Elisha's servant to see the heavenly hosts protecting them (2 Kings 6:17). In the familiar Christmas account, the shepherds saw angels (Luke 2:9-14). In the visions recorded in the book of Revelation, John repeatedly saw angels. Angels are invisible, yet God made it possible for people to see them.

The soul is invisible too. We can't see it. But that doesn't mean it isn't there. The soul is real. We know this for sure, even though we can't see it. We know this by faith in God's Word. Hebrews 11:1 says, "Faith is being sure of what we hope for and certain of what we do not see."

If we could see a person's soul leave the body at death, we would know for sure the precise moment when that person died. But we can't see this. Even if we could, we would not be able to see where the soul went. Even if we could see the soul, we would still not know what we need Scripture to tell us. The Bible tells us where the soul goes at death.

Where does the soul go at death?

In the previous chapter, we learned that at death "the dust returns to the ground it came from, and the spirit returns to God who gave it" (Ecclesiastes 12:7). That doesn't mean that every soul is permitted to enjoy eternal life in heaven. Hebrews 9:27 explains, "Man is destined to die once, and after that to face judgment." The soul departs from the body at death and is immediately judged by God.

Jesus certainly knew this. After he had atoned for sin, Jesus said, "Go into all the world and preach the good news to all creation. Whoever believes and is baptized will be saved, but whoever does not believe will be condemned" (Mark 16:15,16). Jesus wants everyone to hear the good news of salvation. He wants everyone to know the way to heaven, because everyone will be judged. In that judgment, people who believe in him as Savior and are baptized will be saved, and people who do not believe in him will be condemned.

The best known passage in all of Scripture reveals this same truth. Jesus reveals God's amazing plan of salvation in John 3:16-18:

> "God so loved the world that he gave his one and only Son, that whoever believes in him shall not perish but have eternal life. For God did not send his Son into the world to condemn the world, but to save the world through him. Whoever believes in him is not condemned, but whoever does not believe stands condemned already because he has not believed in the name of God's one and only Son."

Jesus said that whoever believes in him will have eternal life. Whoever does not believe in him will perish. In fact, such a person "stands condemned already" (John 3:18), just as a believer is already saved (Ephesians 2:8).

Jesus revealed where the soul goes at death when he talked about the rich man and Lazarus (Luke 16:19-31). When Lazarus died, "the angels carried him to Abraham's side" (verse 22). His soul went to heaven. When the rich man died, his body "was buried," and his soul suddenly appeared "in hell, where he was in torment" (verses 22,23). So at death, a person's soul either goes to heaven or to hell.

The souls of unbelievers go immediately to hell

What our Savior said about the rich man and Lazarus teaches us much. We would do well to study it carefully. Dr. Siegbert Becker wrote:

> Those who find the concept of eternal punishment distasteful, such as the Jehovah's Witnesses, are accustomed to arguing that this passage cannot be used to demonstrate the existence of a place of eternal torment since it is a parable. In reply, it may be said first of all that the Bible never says that this is a parable, and it may well be an account of an event with which Jesus was acquainted because of his omniscience.
>
> The story also does not fit the pattern of parables. The characters in the parables have no names. Instead they speak of "a certain man," "a good Samaritan," "a Pharisee," "a tax collector," "a farmer," etc. But the poor man here has a name. Moreover, parables deal with commonly occurring events in everyday life. Sowing seed, baking bread, selling pearls, picking grapes, inheriting money, celebrating weddings, catching fish: these are the stuff of parables. For that reason parables are often defined as earthly stories with a heavenly meaning. The so-called parable of the rich man and Lazarus hardly fits that pattern. It is more a heavenly story, or a next world story with an earthly meaning.
>
> Finally, even if the story is a parable, this would not give us grounds for saying that it is pure fantasy. Parables regularly deal with things that really happen. Parables are not fables in which plants and animals are personified. Thus we certainly can view the "parable," so-called, of the rich

man and Lazarus as a description of things that actually happen in real life.[3]

From the account of the rich man, we learn that at death the soul of an unbeliever suddenly arrives in hell. Hell is a place of great torment. It is not a neutral holding ground. While he was in hell, the rich man (his soul) experienced pain. Part of his suffering was realizing that he was forever separated from the joys of heaven. He was not granted any relief from suffering, not even one drop of water. He wanted to prevent his brothers from also coming to this place of torment, because human history was continuing while he was in hell. But this request was also denied. His attitude did not change in hell. He still arrogantly regarded Lazarus as an underling. He still had a low opinion of God's Word. He still wanted to call the shots. But he had no power anymore.

At death, the souls of unbelievers go to hell. Jesus plainly says, "Whoever does not believe will be condemned" (Mark 16:16). Certainly, Jesus will condemn all unbelievers (soul and body, after the resurrection) to hell on judgment day. But the souls of unbelievers go to hell immediately.

Sometime before he came out of the tomb on Easter Sunday, Jesus announced his victory to the souls in hell. First Peter 3:18-20 says:

> For Christ died for sins once for all, the righteous for the unrighteous, to bring you to God. He was put to death in the body but made alive by the Spirit, through whom also he went and preached to *the spirits in prison* who disobeyed long ago when God waited patiently in the days of Noah while the ark was being built.

Jesus did not give those spirits a second chance. He announced his victory to them. Colossians 2:15 reveals this mystery, that after Jesus "disarmed the powers and authorities, he made a public spectacle of them, triumphing over them by the cross." Jesus' descent into hell was like a victory parade. It revealed to all of his enemies that he had won.

Of course, the devil and the evil angels must be included in the number of his enemies in hell. The devil and the evil angels are condemned to hell because they sinned against God. The Bible plainly says, "God did not spare angels when they sinned, but sent them to hell, putting them into gloomy dungeons to be held for judgment" (2 Peter 2:4). These angels were created holy but sinned against God, so he sent them to hell. There they are being held for judgment. Jude 6 agrees completely when it speaks of "the angels who did not keep their positions of authority but abandoned their own home—these he has kept in darkness, bound with everlasting chains for judgment on the great Day."

The devil and the evil angels have been condemned to hell, and all people who follow the devil's ways will be condemned to hell. Jude 7 reveals that the devil and the evil angels aren't the only ones suffering eternal punishment. "In a similar way, Sodom and Gomorrah and the surrounding towns gave themselves up to sexual immorality and perversion. They serve as an example of those who suffer the punishment of eternal fire."

This is a very important lesson for us because we live at a time when basic moral principles are quickly eroding. People insist that they have a right to do what God forbids. Sodom and Gomorrah were particularly guilty of the sin of homosexuality, which God regards as sinful perversion. Even the rich man in hell would agree that those who live in sin without repentance need to be warned. These are not neutral, alternative lifestyles. These unrepented sins drive faith out of the heart. God's Word reveals that there will literally be hell to pay. May all repent and look to Jesus for forgiveness before it is too late.

The souls of believers go immediately to heaven

Those who do believe in Jesus as their Savior from sin can look forward to eternal life. *At death, the souls of believers go immediately to heaven.* While Jesus was hanging on the cross, one of the criminals also being crucified had a change of heart. During the course of that day, the Lord brought him to saving faith. The man said, "Jesus, remember me when you come into your kingdom" (Luke 23:42). Jesus knew this man's heart. He knew that this man now had faith. So Jesus said, "I tell you the truth, today you will be with me in paradise" (verse 43). He would be with Jesus in paradise that very day. The criminal hadn't led an outwardly good life. But, as he was dying, he was converted to faith in Jesus. He would die that very day, and that very day he would be with Jesus in heaven.

When Lazarus died, "the angels carried him to Abraham's side" (Luke 16:22). The angels escorted him to heaven, where he was "comforted" (verse 25). Believers go to heaven when they die. There they find comfort, peace, and rest. Isaiah 57:1,2 says, "The righteous perish, and no one ponders it in his heart; devout men are taken away, and no one understands that the righteous are taken away to be spared from evil. Those who walk uprightly enter into peace; they find rest as they lie in death." Sometimes believers die young to be spared from the evil consequences of sin in this world. At death, these believers go straight to heaven and enter into peace and find rest.

Sometimes the troubles and difficulties and sorrows of this sinful world are so great that believers shed tears. When believers go to heaven, God wipes away the tears. Revelation 7:17 says, "God will wipe away every tear from their eyes." And Revelation 21:4 agrees: "He will wipe every tear from their eyes. There will be no more death or mourning or crying or pain, for the old order of things has passed away." The old order of sin and its consequences will be past and gone when we arrive safely in heaven.

So, we can say that death is a blessing for a believer in Jesus. Scripture does. "Blessed are the dead who die in the Lord from now on. . . . They will rest from their labor" (Revelation 14:13). Believers are subject to all sorts of suffering, which may include physical pain, emotional pain, financial hardship, and persecution. Suffering is difficult. The apostle Paul longed to be in heaven. He wrote, "We groan, longing to be clothed with our heavenly dwelling" (2 Corinthians 5:2). Not many verses later, he repeated this thought: "We are confident, I say, and would prefer to be away from the body and at home with the Lord" (verse 8). In another place, he wrote that he was ready and eager to depart from this life, to die and enter heaven, because it is better than this life. "I desire to depart and be with Christ, which is better by far" (Philippians 1:23).

As Stephen the martyr was dying, he knew that as soon as he died his soul would be with Jesus. So, "while they were stoning him, Stephen prayed, 'Lord Jesus, receive my spirit'" (Acts 7:59).

These are wonderful words for Christians to pray at death. When my grandfather was dying, he kept repeating a similar prayer. Like many other Christians before him, and his Savior first, my grandfather commended his soul to the safekeeping of our gracious God, saying, "Father, into your hands I commit my spirit" (Luke 23:46). Maybe one day, I will have the same opportunity to pray that prayer. But really, many millions of believers do this every night when they pray:

> Now I lay me down to sleep;
> I pray Thee, Lord, my soul to keep.
> If I should die before I wake,
> I pray Thee, Lord, my soul to take.

Sure, it is a childhood prayer. But it is an exceedingly good one for adults to pray too. Should we ever consider ourselves too old to pray this way? Jesus says, "I tell you the truth, anyone who will not receive the kingdom of God like a little child will never enter it" (Mark 10:15). May we, with childlike trust, commit our souls to the safekeeping of our loving Savior.

Do people get a second chance after death?

We have learned that, at death, a person's soul goes to heaven or to hell. "Whoever believes and is baptized will be saved, but whoever does not believe will be condemned" (Mark 16:16). No believer would want a second chance after experiencing the joy of eternal life in heaven. But an unbeliever who is condemned to hell must long for a second chance. The rich man in hell certainly would have liked a "do over." But he didn't get a second chance.

No one else gets a second chance either. God's Word says, "Man is destined to die once, and after that to face judgment" (Hebrews 9:27). That judgment is final. There is no appeal. God's judgment is always correct. He knows everything.

Once in hell, no one can cross over to heaven. There is a "great chasm" between heaven and hell, and no one crosses from hell to heaven or from heaven to hell (Luke 16:26). Jesus spoke of hell as "eternal punishment" for a reason (Matthew 25:46). It lasts forever.

What about purgatory?

The Roman Catholic Church does not agree that heaven and hell are the only two destinations after this life. The official *Catechism of the Catholic Church* declares that there is a purgatory.

> All who die in God's grace and friendship, but still imperfectly purified, are indeed assured of their eternal salvation; but after death they undergo purification, so as to achieve the holiness necessary to enter the joy of heaven. The Church gives the name *Purgatory* to this final purification of the elect, which is entirely different from the punishment of the damned. The Church formulated her doctrine of faith on Purgatory especially at the Councils of Florence and Trent.[4]

Another Roman Catholic doctrine book reveals the teaching of the Roman Catholic Church very plainly in a question-and-answer form.

> **What is Purgatory?** Purgatory is a place where souls suffer for a time after death on account of their sins.
>
> **What souls go to Purgatory?** Those souls go to Purgatory that depart this life in venial sin; or that have not fully paid the debt of temporal punishment due to those sins of which the guilt has been forgiven. . . .
>
> **How are we in communion with the souls in Purgatory?** We are in communion with the souls in Purgatory by helping them with our prayers and good works.[5]

This same text defines a venial sin as "an offense which does not kill the soul, yet which displeases God."[6]

One former Roman Catholic member said in our adult instruction class that a local priest plainly told his congregation in a homily, "I believe that I'm going to purgatory, and so are you."

For many centuries the Roman Catholic Church also has spoken of two other destinations after death: the limbo of the fathers and the limbo of children. The limbo of the fathers is for "certain souls who died before the Redemption," when Jesus died on the cross. They were "detained in a place of temporary happiness, awaiting the opening of Heaven by Our Lord."[7] The limbo of children is for "unbaptized children who die before attaining the use of reason, plus mentally handicapped persons who never attained the use of reason."[8] In recent years the teaching of limbo has fallen out of favor within the Roman Catholic Church. Catholic theologians point out that while the Roman Catholic Church has officially declared purgatory to be a doctrine, it never did so with limbo. Limbo, while taught and believed by Roman Catholics for centuries, was officially only a "theological theory" that now is being discarded.

The Bible does not teach the existence of purgatory, limbo, or any other place between heaven and hell. The *Catechism of the Catholic Church* actually points to the unscriptural practice of praying for the dead as one reason for teaching that there is a purgatory.[9] Over the years, Roman Catholic theologians have attempted to appeal to a few Bible passages to support the idea of a purgatory, but none of these teaches that there is a purgatory or limbo after this life.

Not only is there no basis for teaching that there is some place other than heaven and hell where souls go, teaching that there is such a place conflicts with clear Bible passages. There is no safety net between heaven and hell. Jesus says, "Whoever believes and is baptized will be saved, but whoever does not believe will be condemned" (Mark 16:16). There is no need for such a place, "for God so loved the world that he gave his one and only Son, that whoever believes in him shall not perish but have eternal life" (John 3:16).

Luther realized that purgatory was based on a system of salvation by works. He wrote from his own personal experience as a former Roman Catholic: "Some thought that they would never get out of purgatory because, according to the ancient canons, seven years of penance were required for a single mortal sin. Nevertheless, confidence was placed in man's own works of satisfaction."[10]

Basing salvation on our own good works, either totally or only in part, is completely wrong. Romans 3:20 declares, "No one will be declared righteous in his sight by observing the law; rather, through the law we become conscious of sin." No one will get to heaven by trying to obey the law. The law shows us our sins. It cannot save us from sin. So, "we maintain that a man is justified by faith apart from observing the law" (verse 28). And we can pile up the Bible passages to prove that we are not saved by our own good works. Galatians 2:16 boldly states, "A man is not justified by observing the law, but by faith in Jesus Christ. So we, too, have put our faith in Christ Jesus that we may be justified by faith in Christ and not by observing the law, because by observing the law no one will be justified." Galatians 3:11 says, "Clearly no one is justified before God by the law, because, 'The righteous will live by faith.'" And Ephesians 2:8,9 very simply reveals how a person is saved: "For it is by grace you have been saved, through faith—and this not from yourselves, it is the gift of God—not by works, so that no one can boast."

What about reincarnation?

Many people today speak as though reincarnation were true. Essentially, reincarnation is the idea that when a person dies the soul proceeds to a new and different body or becomes a different form of life. According to this way of thinking, one could become a different person, an animal, or even an insect in the next life. Many people today talk about what they did in a past life. This idea of having "past lives" and "future lives" is reincarnation. It has become such a common idea, even some church members wonder if it might be true. It isn't.

The idea of reincarnation originated in Hinduism, although other ancient pagan philosophers also seemed to dabble in these ideas. It isn't difficult to see how people's imaginations could lead them to the concept of reincarnation. People don't want to go out of existence. They want that second chance. It seems to make sense that you could have a second chance, maybe by being someone or something else. But reincarnation is a dangerous false teaching. It conflicts with the clear teaching of Scripture. Hebrews 9:27 declares, "Man is destined to die *once,* and after that to face judgment." The rich man and Lazarus did not become insects or birds, and neither will anyone else. At death, souls go to heaven or hell.

The doctrinal pamphlet *This We Believe* expresses a brief scriptural evaluation of reincarnation based on Hebrews 9:27. "We reject the teaching that the souls of people who have died return to earth in other bodies (reincarnation)."[11]

What about universalism?

Universalism is the false idea that everyone goes to heaven in the end. This false teaching is very common among the most liberal theologians today. People express universalism when they say "he's happier now" after an unbeliever has died. People like to think that their deceased friends and family members have gone to a better place. If your friends and family members happen to be believers in Jesus Christ, they do go to heaven. But if they were not believers when they died, then claiming that they are in a better place isn't true. The Bible gives no support at all for the notion that God will finally take everyone to heaven.

In the Old Testament, we read of what will happen at the end: "Multitudes who sleep in the dust of the earth will awake: some to everlasting life, others to shame and everlasting contempt" (Daniel 12:2) . In the New Testament, Jesus says, "Whoever believes and is baptized will be saved, but whoever does not believe will be condemned" (Mark 16:16).

Only God knows what is in a person's heart. We have to go by a person's confession of faith, which includes his or her words and actions. If we have no reason to think that the deceased was a believer, we really should not say that he or she went to a better place. But if we are not certain that someone died in unbelief, we should not say that the person went to hell either. When matters are doubtful, it is best to be very cautious with our words. Christians should not mislead people into thinking that everyone goes to heaven in the end.

John the Baptist said, "Whoever believes in the Son has eternal life, but whoever rejects the Son will not see life, for God's wrath remains on him" (John 3:36). Jesus is the only way to heaven. He says, "I am the way and the truth and the life. No one comes to the Father except through me" (John 14:6). Acts 4:12 says, "Salvation is found in no one else, for there is no other name under heaven given to men by which we must be saved." Jesus is this world's one and only Savior.

On the basis of these Bible passages, *This We Believe* offers this clear summary:

> We reject universalism, the belief that all people are saved, even those without faith in Christ (John 3:36). We reject pluralism, the belief that there are other ways to salvation besides faith in Christ (John 14:6; Acts 4:12). We reject any teaching that says it does not matter what one believes so long as one has faith in God.[12]

> Though thoughtless thousands choose the road
> That leads the soul away from God,
> This happiness, dear Lord, be mine:
> To live and die entirely thine. (CW 466:1)

3

Moment of Death and
Near-Death Experiences

It happens over and over again in emergency rooms of hospitals all over the world. An ambulance brings in a patient who needs immediate medical attention. Doctors and nurses hurry to try to help, but suddenly a flat line appears on the heart monitor. There is no pulse. The heart has stopped. They frantically attempt to resuscitate the patient. Has the patient already died? How long should they continue trying to revive the patient? Eventually, the heart starts beating again or the doctors and nurses cease their efforts to save the person's life. If the patient does not respond after a certain period of time, they must admit that the patient has died. But how long is that period of time? When are they sure that the patient has died?

From a human perspective, what is the moment of death?
The very instant that someone dies is called the moment of death. But how clear is the moment of death from a human perspective? Can we know for sure? What vital signs would you check to determine the moment of death?

In simpler times, when medical technology was not so advanced, it seemed fairly simple. If a person stopped breathing and had no pulse, the person was considered dead. When there was no longer any breath or heartbeat, doctors could be sure that the patient had died.

To some extent, even today, these two key indicators signal the moment of death. But now technology permits artificial respiration (breathing) and even help with circulation (heartbeat), so that doctors now look to brain function as the key indicator of death. The latest medical technology can often be a great blessing, but it has definitely made it much more difficult to determine the moment of death.

In years gone by, death meant the cessation of the vital signs—heartbeat and breathing. Now doctors realize that death is a process, rather than an event. Life continues even after heartbeat and breathing have stopped. An electric shock can force the heart muscles to work again, and artificial respiration can restart the breathing process. . . . Since different parts of the body die at different rates, scientists and philosophers are still debating when death occurs. The brain usually dies after only four minutes without a supply of oxygen-rich blood. The kidneys, however, can remain "alive" for 30 minutes, and the eye's cornea for up to 6 hours. . . . Many experts now argue that death occurs when the brain dies. Doctors have coined the term "brain death" for this condition, by which they mean irreversible damage to the brain shown by a lack of spontaneous muscular activity . . . and a flat electroencephalogram for more than 30 minutes. (An EEG measures brain wave activity.) From this state, no one has ever been revived.[13]

No one, that is, except those who have really risen from death.

Lazarus was raised after being dead and buried for four days (John 11:38-44). Jesus rose from death on the third day (1 Corinthians 15:3,4). There was no doubt that Lazarus and Jesus had really died. There is some doubt that people who are resuscitated today have really "died." One doctor put it this way:

Both the events at death and the stages of death are debatable. Also debatable is the chosen time to stop our efforts of recovery of the victim. Clinical (reversible) death is said to occur when the heart stops and breathing ceases; biological (irreversible) death occurs when all tissues degenerate beyond any function; legal death occurs when the body shows no response to adequate resuscitative efforts.[14]

Life support

When a patient is on life support, being kept alive by artificial means, even doctors might begin to wonder if the patient is still alive. Grief-stricken families might have to wrestle with the dilemma of whether or not to discontinue life support. In real life, this can be a very difficult question. It is wise to consider life-support questions on a case-by-case basis. If you are ever in this difficult situation, try to obtain as much information as possible from the doctor and seek the advice of your pastor. There are some basic principles that we can draw from God's Word and apply to this question of continuing or ceasing life support.

One very important consideration is *motive*. Why does someone want to remove life support? We do not have the right to determine when others should die. God has given us the Fifth Commandment: "You shall not murder" (Exodus 20:13; also Matthew 19:18; Mark 10:19; Luke 18:20; Romans 13:9). If someone wishes to end or terminate the life of another, that is a sinful motive.

Even if someone is suffering greatly, we never have the right to become involved in mercy killing (euthanasia). If a loving husband kills his wife because she is suffering from cancer, it is still sinful murder. Though his intention might be to spare her from suffering, he has no right to end her life. God says, "You shall not murder."

Only God has the right to decide when people should die. He says, "There is no god besides me. I put to death and I bring to life" (Deuteronomy 32:39). That is one basic principle to keep in mind when approaching end-of-life decisions. We are not to decide when people should die. We are sometimes asked to decide their level of treatment. But their lives are always in God's hands.

Sometimes people speak as though they have the right to decide when they should die. But they don't. Only God has that right. If a person is suffering from cancer and doesn't want to suffer anymore, that person does not have the right to end his or her own life. No one has the right to commit suicide. Although the "right to die" movement claims that each person has that right, God strictly forbids this. Suicide is a sin against the Fifth Commandment. "You shall not murder" yourself!

Believers want God to decide when people should die. This might sound obvious, but when considering questions about life support sometimes even Christians might be tempted to forget this. A believer should say with the psalmist, "I trust in you, O LORD; I say, 'You are my God.' My times are in your hands" (Psalm 31:14,15). Our times are in God's hands!

A person who commits suicide, insisting on the right to determine his or her own time and terms of death, seems to be saying, "I don't trust in you, Lord. You are not my God. My times are in my own hands." That is the very opposite of what the psalmist said. This attitude does not come from faith but from unbelief. We certainly do not want to die in unbelief!

Cancer and other diseases are awful. We dare not underestimate how difficult terminal diseases can be. They are among the most horrible consequences of sin. But, no matter how bad it is, we never have the right to take our own lives.

Active and passive euthanasia

The term *euthanasia* comes from the Greek word for "good death." *Active euthanasia* is mercy killing. It is terminating human life by direct intervention. One example is when a husband decides his wife has suffered enough and kills her. Whether he uses a pillow to suffocate or a lethal injection to poison, it is still murder in God's sight. *Passive euthanasia* is more subtle because it involves being passive (not active) toward a suffering patient. One example is attempting to hasten death by withdrawing food and drink, so that the suffering patient dies more quickly of starvation.

Biblical Principles

1. Only God has the right to end human life.*

2. We do not have the right to decide when we or others should die.

(*He does authorize government to wage just wars and to carry out capital punishment. See the scriptural exposition of the Fourth and Fifth Commandments in Luther's Small Catechism.)

Some applications of these principles

After carefully reviewing the two basic principles from God's Word printed above, let us now draw some applications to end-of-life situations.

1. If we are asked to determine the level of health care in an end-of-life situation, our role is not to decide when others should die. We leave that decision up to God.

2. Our role is to use the best advice, information, and Christian judgment to determine the appropriate level of medical treatment based on what seems to be God's will in this case.

3. We should not seek to end life before it is God's will.

4. We should not seek to prolong life longer than it is God's will.

5. God can keep people alive without medical help if it is his will.

6. God can end people's lives even if they are on life support if it is his will.

7. Sometimes there may not be a clear right or wrong answer as to whether a certain level of medical care should be maintained or terminated.

8. It is essential that we approach each case with the proper motive. As Christians, we want to remember that this person's life is in the Lord's hands. We want his will to be done.

It is not always wrong to remove life support or even a feeding tube. As a basic rule of thumb, we will want to keep a feeding tube in place because it supplies the basic human need of food and water to a patient. Yet, there can be an exception even to that basic rule of thumb. For example, a feeding tube could be removed if a person's body is no longer able to digest food. In that case, it would be futile or even harmful to continue to use it. Breathing machines (ventilators, respirators) can be very useful to help people breathe as they recover from some inability to breathe normally. If the patient does not recover normal breathing, a difficult decision might have to be made.

We need to seek the best information we can from the medical professionals. A pastor can provide helpful advice, with guidance from God's Word. Believers need to remain focused on the basic principle that *only God has the right to decide when a patient should die*. A believer will pray, "I trust in you, O LORD; I say, 'You are my God.' My times are in your hands" (Psalm 31:14,15). Our loved one's times are in his hands too.

We should not seek to prolong life longer than God intends, just as we should not seek to end life before God intends. Sometimes it is not very clear what we should do. When in doubt, keep in mind that the person's life is in God's hands. He can keep that person alive without life support if he wants. And he can end that person's life even if the person is on life support. So, we must never think that we are in the position of deciding when a patient should die. That is God's decision to make. If we are asked, we are simply to determine the type of medical treatment the patient is to receive.

After seeking the best information from the doctor and the best advice from our pastor, we will do well to pray, "This person's life is in your hands, Lord." This is the proper motive when approaching these difficult decisions. God is still in control. After all of this, the decision might be to remove the breathing machine and place the person in God's hands. If the medical professionals slowly wean the patient from the breathing machine, it can happen that the patient will continue breathing for some time. It could be minutes, hours, days, or even years.

Many of us can still remember the case of Karen Ann Quinlan from the 1970s. She was kept alive on life support after falling into a coma from an overdose of drugs and alcohol. Her parents wanted to remove life support but needed to obtain the government's permission in court. Day after day the legal battle appeared in the news. Finally, Karen's parents received permission. But an amazing thing happened when life support was removed. She didn't die. Karen continued to live for nine more years.'

God is able to sustain life with his power if he is not ready for a person to die. That doesn't mean that we should be careless about these difficult decisions. It does mean that we have every reason to approach the decision with this attitude in mind: "I trust in you, O Lord; I say, 'You are my God.' My times are in your hands" (Psalm 31:14,15).

From God's perspective, what is the moment of death?

God always knows the moment of death. The moment of death is always clear from God's perspective. Ecclesiastes 12:7 says, "The dust returns to the ground it came from, and the spirit returns to God who gave it." God knows the precise moment when the soul departs from the body. From God's perspective, the moment of death is when the soul finally leaves the body. "The body without the spirit is dead" (James 2:26). If we could see and know what God sees and knows, we would never be in doubt about whether or not a person died.

What can we say about near-death experience (NDE)?

Dr. Raymond A. Moody Jr. might have invented the phrase "near-death experience" in 1975 when he claimed in his book *Life after Life* that there is a "striking similarity" among the accounts of these experiences, though "no two of them are precisely identical." He described a typical experience of near-death this way:

> A man is dying and, as he reaches the point of greatest physical distress, he hears himself pronounced dead by his doctor. He begins to hear an uncomfortable noise, a loud ringing or buzzing, and at the same time feels himself moving very rapidly through a long dark tunnel. After this, he suddenly finds himself outside of his own physical body, but still in the immediate physical environment, and he sees his own body from a distance, as though he is a spectator. He watches the resuscitation attempt from this unusual vantage point and is in a state of emotional upheaval.

> After a while, he collects himself and becomes more accustomed to his odd condition. He notices that he still has a "body," but one of a very different nature and with very different powers from the physical body he has left

behind. Soon other things begin to happen. Others come to meet and to help him. He glimpses the spirits of relatives and friends who have already died, and a loving, warm spirit of a kind he has never encountered before—a being of light—appears before him. This being asks him a question, nonverbally, to make him evaluate his life and helps him along by showing him a panoramic, instantaneous playback of the major events of his life. At some point he finds himself approaching some sort of barrier or border, apparently representing the limit between earthly life and the next life. Yet, he finds that he must go back to the earth, that the time for his death has not yet come. At this point he resists, for by now he is taken up with his experience in the afterlife and does not want to return. He is overwhelmed by intense feelings of joy, love, and peace. Despite his attitude, though, he somehow reunites with his physical body and lives.

Later he tries to tell others, but he has trouble doing so. In the first place, he can find no human words adequate to describe these unearthly episodes. He also finds that others scoff, so he stops telling other people. Still, the experience affects his life profoundly, especially his views about death and its relationship to life.[15]

Dr. Moody described only pleasant experiences in his book, but he did not consider that an omission. Two years later (1977), Dr. Moody wrote: "It remains true that in the mass of material I have collected no one has ever described to me a state like the archetypical hell."[16]

In the very next year (1978), Dr. Maurice S. Rawlings sharply disagreed. As a cardiologist dealing with coronary patients, Rawlings had "many opportunities to resuscitate people who have clinically died" and reported that "an interview immediately after patients are revived reveals as many bad experiences as good ones."[17] He wrote:

Let me again emphasize that contrary to most published life-after-death cases, not all death experiences are good. Hell also exists! After my own realization of this fact I started collecting accounts of unpleasant cases that other investigators apparently had missed. This has happened, I think, because the investigators, normally psychiatrists, have never *resuscitated* a patient. They have not had the opportunity to be on the scene. The unpleasant experiences in my study have turned out to be at least as frequent as the pleasant ones.[18]

He describes one key incident in which a 48-year-old man went into cardiac arrest and dropped dead in his office. The man's heart had stopped. Dr. Rawlings and the nurses initiated emergency medical treatment to restart the man's heart. Occasionally, it would start again, only to stop. "Each time he regained heartbeat and respiration, the patient screamed, 'I am in hell!' He was terrified and pleaded with me to help him. I was scared to death. . . . It terrified me enough to write this book."[19] When he asked the patient, only a couple days later, about what he had seen in hell, the patient could no longer recall the experience.[20]

Rawlings' book reveals that not all of the so-called near-death experiences are warm, happy experiences of light and peace and joy. Many patients seem to experience something like hell. Dr. Rawlings eventually began reading the Bible to learn more about hell and how to avoid it.

Rawlings' description of a typical near-death experience is, in many ways, similar to Dr. Moody's, except that Rawlings insists that the new "environment may be inexpressibly wonderful, frequently a rolling meadow or a beautiful city; or it may be inexpressibly horrible, frequently a dungeon or a huge cave."[21] Interestingly, Rawlings adds, "I don't know of any 'good' out-of-the-body experiences that have resulted from suicide."[22]

As we consider these near-death experiences, we must wonder if these people are really experiencing heaven and hell or not. But to answer that, we need to know if these people really have died. Dr. Rawlings explains:

> Reversible death (or clinical death) is that type of death that is potentially recoverable by restarting the heart and lungs. The brain and underlying vital tissues have not yet died; when the brain and vital tissues die, irreversible death (or tissue death) has occurred. Resuscitation from reversible death should certainly not be confused with resurrection from irreversible death. One requires training; the other a miracle![23]

In other words, these people have not really experienced resurrections from death. So, have they really died, then?

Not all resuscitated patients have these experiences. Dr. Rawlings claims that "of those who are retrieved from death by restarting the heartbeat and breathing, only about twenty percent volunteer experiences of a life beyond."[24] Other research indicates "that between 27 and 42 percent of resuscitated patients report an NDE."[25] And out of that group, Rawlings claims that roughly half have good experiences and half have bad ones.[26]

So, are these people really experiencing heaven or hell? Or, is it more likely that these experiences are caused by the mind's reaction to the unique stresses of dying?

Dr. Susan Blackmore describes the common near-death experience as "the brain's last fling" because she believes it is "a psychological trick, played by the dying brain on the consciousness in order to lessen the trauma of dying."[27]

If she is correct, it might be related to out-of-body experiences in which people feel themselves separating from and leaving their physical bodies. They seem to be able to look at themselves and what is happening from a location outside their own bodies. This is very difficult to understand and explain, but I have heard it described to me by a believer who did not know what to make of it (nor did I). "Out-of-body experiences are not necessarily associated with the onset of death, however. They have been reported after a blow to the head, during a period of unconsciousness, in sleep, or at times of acute mental or physical stress."[28]

The descriptions of other cases of this match the one I am familiar with. It is difficult to distinguish these cases from mental telepathy or extrasensory perception (ESP). Dr. Siegbert Becker admitted that it could be . . .

> . . . that there are powers within the human mind which are as yet not fully understood but which make it possible for certain persons to transcend the limits of space and time. . . . Scientists who are confronted with evidence of such occurrences generally explain them as being evidence for the existence of such as yet little understood mental capacities, which are natural but paranormal.[29]

Have you ever had a sense of déjà vu? If so, how did you understand it? There are elaborate explanations for this, but the truth is that nobody really knows. Could it be that the near-death experiences people seem to remember are similar?

Some experts claim that people's near-death experiences seem to be affected by religion and culture.[30] If that is the case, might some of these experiences be related to imagination or dreams? "Some researchers have suggested that it is simply a neuro-physiological phenomenon, a piece of clever and elaborate mental programming."[31]

Might these experiences be the result of what happens when the brain dies in phases? Parts of the brain that survive longer might produce imaginary experiences, hallucinations, to compensate for the lack of incoming sensory information. There are elaborate explanations for why the brain might imagine tunnel images, but how can someone witness his or her own resuscitation?

> Dr. Blackmore suggests that, in such a "dying" state, the mind is deprived of its usual levels of sensory input and starts asking questions. Who am I? Where am I? In an attempt to answer these questions, it turns to the memory. Using information stored in its memory bank, such as images of a hospital room and medical procedure, it creates a vision of what it believes reality to be. As hearing is the last sense to deteriorate, this vision of reality may also incorporate some "real" sound input. Dr. Blackmore is the first to admit that this theory does not explain the claims of researchers that some near-deathers are able to describe in great detail events and environments that they have not seen or experienced before.[32]

Dr. Blackmore specifically mentions that hearing is the last sense to deteriorate. Pastors often proclaim the gospel to people who are dying, even if there is no response, with the understanding that hearing is one of the last senses to depart. We hope that these people are hearing the saving, encouraging gospel of Jesus Christ, even if they cannot indicate that they hear it. A person in a coma might even recall conversations in the room. Dr. Rawlings agrees: "Some who survive reversible death have total recall of any conversation in the room that took place during their resuscitation. Perhaps this is because hearing is one of the last senses to leave the body in death. I don't know . . ."[33]

Note his last three words carefully. We cannot be certain of all aspects of these experiences, but we can be certain of everything God tells us in the Bible. The Bible tells us that a few people really rose from the dead. They probably fall into a different category. None of the people with near-death experiences had a flat electroencephalogram for more than 30 minutes. But that would have been the case for those who really rose from the dead (if they would have had that technology).

The Bible tells us that we as human beings have two parts—a body and a soul, and we know it is possible for the soul to exist apart from the body. But we normally associate this separation with death. The Bible also says that Satan "masquerades as an angel of light" (2 Corinthians 11:14). If an unbeliever has a positive near-death experience and is reinforced in his or her unbelief and impenitence, we know that does not come from God. It could be the work of the devil. The Bible does not tell us if Lazarus (John 11:43,44), the daughter of Jairus (Mark 5:41,42), the young man of Nain (Luke 7:14,15), or all the saints who were raised on Good Friday (Matthew 27:52) ever told about their experiences of the soul apart from the body, or even if they could remember what it was like. But we do read these words of Christ: "No one has ever gone into heaven except the one who came from heaven—the Son of Man" (John 3:13). He is the one to listen to.

What about deathbed visions?

From time to time, pastors, family members, and others who sit with the dying may notice that sometimes Christians seem to see heavenly visions just before they die. Some, including this author, have witnessed this phenomenon at the deathbed of Christians. As believers approach the very moment of death, they might suddenly seem to see something that no one else can see, smile, and say something like "It's so beautiful and peaceful!" just before closing their eyes in death. Or they might seem to see a person, perhaps an angel or Jesus. They might even ask if you see what they see. After privately pondering this phenomenon for years, I found this description to be consistent with what I have witnessed:

> The 19th-century "deathbed vision," a widely reported phenomenon, was examined by researchers of the period much as the NDE [near-death experience] is today. At that time, most people died at home surrounded by their families. . . . Families frequently reported that the dying person had described other-worldly scenes before passing on. . . . During deathbed visions, unlike NDE's, the patient was still very much alive. Daisy [a girl whose case was described] said clearly that she could see her living relatives at the bedside and the spirit beings simultaneously: "I can see you all and I can see them there at the same time."[34]

Perhaps God occasionally grants this to dying believers as further encouragement. We have no certain information about this, but we know what Stephen the martyr saw as he was dying. "Stephen, full of the Holy Spirit, looked up to heaven and saw the glory of God, and Jesus standing at the right hand of God. 'Look,' he said, 'I see heaven open and the Son of Man standing at the right hand of God'" (Acts 7:55,56). Receiving this genuine heavenly vision just before dying must have been very encouraging for Stephen. He even invited others to see the same sight when he said, "Look."

Perhaps a little more mysterious is the inspired account of the apostle Paul, who wrote about an experience he had but did not fully understand:

> I must go on boasting. Although there is nothing to be gained, I will go on to visions and revelations from the Lord. I know a man in Christ who fourteen years ago was caught up to the third heaven. Whether it was in the body or out of the body I do not know—God knows. And I know that this man—whether in the body or apart from the body I do not know, but God knows—was caught up to paradise. He heard inexpressible things, things that man is not permitted to tell. (2 Corinthians 12:1-4)

The third heaven is the same as *paradise* in these verses. We would just say heaven. What Paul describes is something of a mystery, but it is revealed in Scripture for our learning. As we consider near-death experiences and deathbed visions and wonder about these, we can find some direction in these inspired words: "Whether it was in the body or out of the body I do not know—God knows." If the inspired apostle Paul was not sure about this situation, it is acceptable for us to be unsure about some aspects of near-death experiences or deathbed visions. We should not believe anything contrary to the Bible, because God never lies to us.

We may not all have near-death experiences or deathbed visions, but we can be thankful for the absolutely reliable vision of heaven afforded to the apostle John and recorded for us in the Bible:

> After this I looked and there before me was a great multitude that no one could count, from every nation, tribe, people and language, standing before the throne and in front of the Lamb. They were wearing white robes and were holding palm branches in their hands. And they

cried out in a loud voice: "Salvation belongs to our God, who sits on the throne, and to the Lamb."

All the angels were standing around the throne and around the elders and the four living creatures. They fell down on their faces before the throne and worshiped God, saying: "Amen! Praise and glory and wisdom and thanks and honor and power and strength be to our God for ever and ever. Amen!"

Then one of the elders asked me, "These in white robes—who are they, and where did they come from?"

I answered, "Sir, you know."

And he said, "These are they who have come out of the great tribulation; they have washed their robes and made them white in the blood of the Lamb. Therefore, "they are before the throne of God and serve him day and night in his temple; and he who sits on the throne will spread his tent over them. Never again will they hunger; never again will they thirst. The sun will not beat upon them, nor any scorching heat. For the Lamb at the center of the throne will be their shepherd; he will lead them to springs of living water. And God will wipe away every tear from their eyes." (Revelation 7:9-17)

One day, we believers will be there. "Whoever believes and is baptized will be saved, but whoever does not believe will be condemned" (Mark 16:16).

4

Hell: Bible Definition and Terms

Moses and the prophets did not write the Old Testament in the English language. The Old Testament was written in Hebrew and Aramaic. The apostles did not write the New Testament in English either. They wrote in the Greek language. When we read the Bible today, we read translations. Translation is not as simple as taking one word in Hebrew and giving it an exact term in English. Sometimes the original languages had more than one term for a concept that corresponds with only one term in English. It is commonly known that the Greek language has more than one term for *love*. In a similar way, there was not just one term in Hebrew or Greek for *hell*.

NIV uses the word *hell* to translate three different Greek terms in the New Testament: *gehenna, hades,* and *tartarus.* The KJV and the New King James Version (NKJV) some-times translate the Hebrew term *sheol* as "hell," but the NIV never does. The context in each passage helps us to determine how these terms are being used. In some cases with *hades* and *sheol,* conservative Bible teachers don't always agree on exactly the best ways to translate.

Gehenna

The Greek term *gehenna* appears 12 times in the New Testament. Every time, the NIV translates it as *hell.* When you read the term *hell* in the NIV, you can be sure that it is from the Greek term *gehenna,* with only two exceptions (Luke 16:23 and 2 Peter 2:4). Those two exceptions both describe hell before judgment day. *Gehenna* seems to be the term for *hell* after judgment day.

Gehenna originated from the Old Testament terms for "the Valley of Ben Hinnom," a valley south of Jerusalem. In this valley, wicked people sacrificed their children (2 Kings 23:10; 2 Chronicles 28:3). Eventually this valley became known as the place where God would punish the wicked (Jeremiah 7:32; 19:6,7).

Jesus talks about hell more than anyone else in Scrip-ture. Since he is the eternal Son of God, he is able to speak about hell with ultimate authority. He lovingly warns people about the terrible punishment of hell. Jesus commonly used the term *gehenna* for hell. He said:

> If your right eye causes you to sin, gouge it out and throw it away. It is better for you to lose one part of your body than for your whole body to be thrown into hell *[gehenna]*. And if your right hand causes you to sin, cut it off and throw it away. It is better for you to lose one part of your

body than for your whole body to go into hell *[gehenna]*. (Matthew 5:29,30)

God can throw a person's body into hell *[gehenna]*. Jesus is talking about hell after the resurrection on the Last Day. He does the same in Matthew 10:28, when he says, "Do not be afraid of those who kill the body but cannot kill the soul. Rather, be afraid of the One who can destroy both soul and body in hell *[gehenna]*."

Jesus warned the Pharisees and teachers of the law that they were on the road to hell. He sharply rebuked them saying, "You snakes! You brood of vipers! How will you escape being condemned to hell?" (Matthew 23:33).

We also read of hell in the epistles. James 3:6 uses the term *gehenna* for hell when teaching about controlling the tongue. "The tongue also is a fire, a world of evil among the parts of the body. It corrupts the whole person, sets the whole course of his life on fire, and is itself set on fire by hell."

Hades/Sheol

The Greek term *hades* appears ten times in the New Testament Scriptures. Of these ten appearances of *hades*, the NIV translates with *hell* only once. That one case is Luke 16:23, where the rich man's soul was in torment. We know the rich man only had a soul at this time because his body had been buried and his brothers were still living.

> The rich man also died and was buried. In hell *[hades]*, where he was in torment, he looked up and saw Abraham far away, with Lazarus by his side. . . . "I beg you, father, send Lazarus to my father's house, for I have five brothers. Let him warn them, so that they will not also come to this place of torment." (Luke 16:22,23,27,28)

Five times, the NIV simply transliterates with the word *hades*. Twice, it uses *depths*. And, twice it renders it *grave*. The Septuagint (Greek translation of the Old Testament) generally used the Greek term *hades* to translate the Hebrew term *sheol*. These two terms have very similar meanings.

The Hebrew term *sheol* can mean "the grave," "the realm of the dead," or "hell." The context of each passage helps us understand how this term is being used. Sometimes, it is difficult to be certain of the precise nuance of this term. While the NIV never uses *hell* to translate the Hebrew term *sheol,* the two passages that follow reveal examples where *sheol* probably should be translated as "hell": "For a fire is kindled by My anger, And shall burn to the lowest *hell [sheol];* It shall consume the earth with her increase, And set on fire the foundations of the mountains" (Deuteronomy 32:22 NKJV). And "If I ascend into *heaven,* You *are* there; If I make my bed in *hell [sheol],* behold, You *are there*" (Psalm 139:8 NKJV).

God is everywhere, even in the farthest extremes of heaven and hell. That seems to be the point of Psalm 139:8. Though the spirits (souls) in hell are separated from God's grace and blessing, God remains omnipresent even in hell, justly punishing the wicked. The clue that *sheol* seems to mean "hell" here comes from the context, where the sharpest contrast is between heaven and hell.

Compare Matthew 11:23, where the NIV translation of the Greek term *hades* seems unfortunately weak. The sharpest contrast is between heaven and hell, not merely skies and depths. "And you, Capernaum, will you be lifted up to *the skies* [KJV: heaven]? No, you will go down to *the depths* [KJV: hell; Greek: *hades*]. If the miracles that were performed in you had been performed in Sodom, it would have remained to this day."

The term *hades* also describes the base of the devil's power. Jesus said, "I tell you that you are Peter, and on this rock I will build my church, and the gates of Hades will not overcome it" (Matthew 16:18). The devil's power will not overcome the church of all believers in Jesus. Jesus holds the power over the devil, death, and hell. He says, "I am the Living One; I was dead, and behold I am alive for ever and ever! And I hold the keys of death and Hades" (Revelation 1:18).

In Revelation 6:8, death and Hades are described as if they were persons: "I looked, and there before me was a pale horse! Its rider was named Death, and Hades was following close behind him." Clearly, death and Hades are closely connected. We know what death is, but what is Hades? Revelation 20:13,14 offers a clue: "The sea gave up the dead that were in it, and death and Hades gave up the dead that were in them, and each person was judged according to what he had done. Then death and Hades were thrown into the lake of fire. The lake of fire is the second death." The lake of fire and the second death are hell after judgment day. Hades seems to be the place where the souls of unbelievers go before judgment day. Recall that this was the location of the rich man in hell. Siegbert Becker writes in his commentary on Revelation: "It has been suggested that perhaps Hades is 'hell' as the abode of the souls of the unbelievers while they exist separated from the body and that the lake of fire is 'hell' as the place of eternal torment for body and soul. That explanation is as good as any."[35]

Tartarus

The last Greek term for hell, *tartarus*, appears only once in the New Testament Scriptures. The New Testament actually uses the verb that means to throw into *tartarus*. *Tartarus* is a term in Greek mythology for a deep, dark abyss. By inspiration, the apostle Peter adopted this term and used it for hell in 2 Peter 2:4, "For if God did not spare angels when they sinned, but sent them to hell *[tartarus]*, putting them into gloomy dungeons to be held for judgment." *Tartarus*, or hell, is the place where God sent the evil angels after they fell into sin to be held until judgment day.

The Bible's definition of hell

If we search the Scriptures for a definition of hell, we repeatedly find passages that talk about eternal separation from God's gracious presence. Jesus will be the judge of all people at the end, on the Last Day. Jesus says that he will condemn unbelievers: "Then I will tell them plainly, 'I never knew you. Away from me, you evil-doers!'" (Matthew 7:23). The words "away from me" describe eternal separation from our Savior's gracious presence. At the end, unbelievers "will be thrown outside, into the darkness, where there will be weeping and gnashing of teeth" (8:12). They will not be permitted to enjoy heaven and eternal pleasures. They will be thrown outside, where they will be eternally separated from heaven.

On the Last Day, Jesus will appear. Unbelievers should rightly be afraid, because "he will say to those on his left, 'Depart from me, you who are cursed, into the eternal fire prepared for the devil and his angels'" (Matthew 25:41). These will be the worst words anyone could ever hear, when Jesus condemns the unbelievers saying, "Depart from me" to be punished in the "eternal fire."

Many people say that a loving God would never condemn anyone to hell. That is false. God is loving, but he is
also just. Sense the finality of these words:

> God is just: He will pay back trouble to those who trouble
> you and give relief to you who are troubled, and to us as
> well. This will happen when the Lord Jesus is revealed
> from heaven in blazing fire with his powerful angels.
> He will punish those who do not know God and do not
> obey the gospel of our Lord Jesus. They will be punished
> with everlasting destruction and shut out from the pres-
> ence of the Lord and from the majesty of his power.
> (2 Thessalonians 1:6-9)

Once again, we see the definition of hell in the words
"shut out from the presence of the Lord." He will carry out
this just punishment on all unbelievers, because "God is
just." This is not debatable, doubtful, or uncertain. God is
just. He will punish the wicked.

Jesus warns unbelievers repeatedly, "There will be weeping there, and gnashing of teeth, when you see Abraham,
Isaac and Jacob and all the prophets in the kingdom of
God, but you yourselves thrown out" (Luke 13:28). The
words "thrown out" remind us that hell is eternal separation from God's gracious presence. It is the very opposite
of heaven.

Condemnation

Hell is God's *condemnation* of those who do evil. Jesus
very clearly reveals who will be condemned: "Whoever
believes and is baptized will be saved, but whoever does not
believe will be condemned" (Mark 16:16). God will condemn unbelievers to eternal punishment. They will receive
his divine judgment on sin and unbelief. Jesus says, "Those
who have done evil will rise to be condemned" on the Last

Day (John 5:29). Condemnation is God's just judgment on sin and righteous punishment of sinners.

Make no mistake about it. We all deserve God's condemnation because we are all sinners. We inherited sin from our ancestors going all the way back to Adam and Eve. Yet Jesus came to rescue us from this condemnation. He saved us and gave us salvation as a free gift. "The gift of God is not like the result of the one man's sin: The judgment followed one sin and brought condemnation, but the gift followed many trespasses and brought justification. Consequently, just as the result of one trespass was condemnation for all men, so also the result of one act of righteousness was justification that brings life for all men" (Romans 5:16,18).

The result is clear and plain. Romans 8:1 declares, "Therefore, there is now no condemnation for those who are in Christ Jesus." Thanks to Jesus, we believers will not be condemned.

But unbelievers will be condemned. Unbelieving false teachers seem to thrive in this world, but they will be condemned. Second Peter 2:3 says, "In their greed these teachers will exploit you with stories they have made up. Their condemnation has long been hanging over them."

Jude 4 describes these false teachers in a very similar way: "Certain men whose condemnation was written about long ago have secretly slipped in among you. They are godless men, who change the grace of our God into a license for immorality and deny Jesus Christ our only Sovereign and Lord." The media often report the sayings of false teachers. These false teachers seem so influential and prosperous now. They claim that Jesus was just a man. They insist that homosexuality is an acceptable lifestyle. We would do well always to remember how things will turn out in the end. Jesus will be the judge of all, and he will condemn all unbelievers. Many prominent false teachers will be revealed as unbelievers and condemned.

Punishment

Hell is punishment, not discipline. God disciplines those he loves, teaching them a lesson that might be temporarily painful. But God punishes unbelievers. On the Last Day, "they will go away to eternal punishment" (Matthew 25:46). Hell is not temporary punishment, like a prison term after which the criminal might be freed. Hell is eternal punishment. Scripture describes it as "the punishment of eternal fire" (Jude 7).

"Hell on the cross"

Jesus suffered the punishment we deserved when he died on the cross as our substitute. First, he lived a perfect life. Then our Savior went to the cross to suffer and die as the atoning sacrifice for all sinners. "The LORD has laid on him the iniquity of us all" (Isaiah 53:6). As Jesus was paying the full penalty of our sins, he cried out with a loud voice, "My God, my God, why have you forsaken me?" (Matthew 27:46). Jesus was suffering the punishment of God's wrath against sin. Jesus was even forsaken by his heavenly Father because of our sins. That is the punishment of hell. So, Jesus suffered the torment of hell on the cross.

Many think about the physical pain and torture of dying by crucifixion. But many criminals died that same terrible death. What was unique about Jesus' suffering was that, invisibly, he was also suffering the divine punishment we deserved for our sins. He was forsaken by God in our place. We cannot understand this. But thank God that it happened. May we praise Jesus forever, because this is how he paid for our sins! He suffered the torment of hell so that we believers would never have to.

Residents of hell

There are many who must suffer in hell forever. God created hell as the place of punishment for "the devil and his angels" (Matthew 25:41). Satan and all of the evil angels suffer the agony of hell forever. Since these angels are spirits, the punishment was made particularly for them.

"If God did not spare angels when they sinned, but sent them to hell, putting them into gloomy dungeons to be held for judgment" (2 Peter 2:4), he will not spare unbelieving people who follow in the devil's wicked ways. The souls of unbelievers suffer in hell too. The rich man's soul went to hell as soon as he died (Luke 16:23).

Jesus says, "Whoever believes and is baptized will be saved, but whoever does not believe will be condemned" (Mark 16:16). We should not question why God sends unbelievers to hell. We should praise God for providing a way out by sending his Son, Jesus, to be our Savior.

> "God so loved the world that he gave his one and only Son, that whoever believes in him shall not perish but have eternal life. For God did not send his Son into the world to condemn the world, but to save the world through him. Whoever believes in him is not condemned, but whoever does not believe stands condemned already because he has not believed in the name of God's one and only Son." Whoever believes in the Son has eternal life, but whoever rejects the Son will not see life, for God's wrath remains on him. (John 3:16-18,36)

God's wrath remains on unbelievers who live in sin without repentance. The inspired apostle Paul wrote, "Do you not know that the wicked will not inherit the kingdom of God? Do not be deceived: Neither the sexually immoral nor idolaters nor adulterers nor male prostitutes nor homosexual offenders nor thieves nor the greedy nor drunkards nor slanderers nor swindlers will inherit the kingdom of God" (1 Corinthians 6:9,10). People who live in sins like these without repenting will be lost.

Many today speak and act as though this will not happen. Do not be deceived! Scripture warns everyone, "Let no one deceive you with empty words, for because of such things God's wrath comes on those who are disobedient" (Ephesians 5:6). The wicked, disobedient unbelievers will be kept out of heaven. They will be eternal residents of hell. Revelation 22:15 describes them as "those who practice magic arts, the sexually immoral, the murderers, the idolaters and everyone who loves and practices falsehood." May we daily renounce and repent of our sins, trusting in Christ's forgiveness.

Location of hell

From time to time, people wonder where hell is. Hell is a place, but we cannot locate it on a map. The rich man in hell did not want his five brothers to be condemned to "this place of torment" (Luke 16:28). Hell is a place of torment. Somehow Jesus went there before he came out of the tomb on Easter Sunday. Jesus descended into hell. God's Word says, "He went and preached to the spirits in prison" (1 Peter 3:19). He went to that place of torment, hell. But where is it?

Some people think of hell as being under the ground. Philippians 2:10 tells us, "At at the name of Jesus every knee should bow, in heaven and on earth and under the earth." Many interpreters consider "under the earth" as a reference to the inhabitants of hell. Certainly, everyone will have to acknowledge that Jesus Christ is Lord and bow the knee. This is also true of those who never wanted him to be the King and those who would not believe in him. But, this verse does not necessarily locate hell on a map. The point is that every knee should bow to Jesus.

It is safest to cling to the Bible truth that hell is a place where the devil, the evil angels, and the unbelievers suffer forever, wherever it is. We should not be as concerned about locating hell as we are of avoiding it. Believe in Jesus Christ as your Savior from sin, and you'll never have to go to that terrible place of torment.

> Jesus, your blood and righteousness
> My beauty are, my glorious dress;
> Mid flaming worlds, in these arrayed,
> With joy shall I lift up my head.

> When from the dust of death I rise
> To claim my mansion in the skies,
> E'en then this shall be all my plea:
> Jesus has lived and died for me. (CW 376:1,5)

5

The Bible's Description
of the Suffering of Hell

What is it like in hell? In the last chapter, we saw that the suffering of hell involves being separated from God's grace and blessing. Everyone in hell is deprived of the joys of heaven. Yet hell involves even more excruciating torment. Scripture describes the suffering of hell with very vivid words.

Fire

God's Word often speaks of the eternal fire of hell. Isaiah 66:24 reveals that the fire of hell will not "be quenched." It will last forever. John the Baptist called it "unquenchable fire" (Matthew 3:12). Our Lord Jesus says that all evildoers would be thrown into "the fiery furnace" (Matthew 13:42). On judgment day, Jesus will be the judge. He will say to the unbelievers, "Depart from me, you who are cursed, into the eternal fire prepared for the devil and his angels" (25:41).

Again and again, the Scriptures warn us that the fiery punishment of hell never ends. For example, our Savior says, "If your hand causes you to sin, cut it off. It is better for you to enter life maimed than with two hands to go into hell, where the fire never goes out" (Mark 9:43). The fire never goes out. The punishment of hell is relentless. It never stops.

This is the just and final punishment for God's wicked enemies. Revelation 21:8 reveals how things will turn out for all unbelievers: "The cowardly, the unbelieving, the vile, the murderers, the sexually immoral, those who practice magic arts, the idolaters and all liars—their place will be in the fiery lake of burning sulfur. This is the second death."

How should we think of this fire? Is it physical fire, like the kind that burns in a fireplace? Or is this just a metaphor, mere picture language, for the torment of hell? Physical fire consumes objects. On judgment day, the elements will melt and everything will be destroyed by fire (2 Peter 3:10,12). Physical fire can be extinguished. By comparison, the eternal fire of hell burns but never goes out. It never completely consumes the damned. It keeps on tormenting them. We would not expect physical fire to affect evil spirits and the souls of unbelievers. This leads some people to claim that this fire is just a metaphor for the suffering of hell.

Yet there are reasons why we should think of this as real fire. God could make physical fire that would burn and torment spirits. But God could also make special fire that is real and yet not exactly like the physical fire we are used to. Whatever it is, hellfire clearly torments evil spirits and the souls of unbelievers. It was real enough to the rich man in hell. He said, "I am in agony in this fire" (Luke 16:24). Notice that there is a distinction between his agony and the fire. For the rich man, the fire of hell was not just a metaphor. It was real fire that caused him agony and pain and torture. He wanted relief but didn't receive it. May we never find out what this fire is really like from personal experience!

Torment

If the rich man could have returned from hell to deliver a lecture on the sufferings of hell, he would have had plenty to say! Unfortunately for him, he could not escape. But God's Word reveals everything that we need to know about the suffering of hell. Let's consider now what it is really like to be in hell. We begin with our Savior's account of the rich man and poor Lazarus (Luke 16:19-31):

> There was a rich man who was dressed in purple and fine linen and lived in luxury every day. At his gate was laid a beggar named Lazarus, covered with sores and longing to eat what fell from the rich man's table. Even the dogs came and licked his sores.

> The time came when the beggar died and the angels carried him to Abraham's side. The rich man also died and was buried. In hell, where he was in *torment*, he looked up and saw Abraham far away, with Lazarus by his side. So he called to him, "Father Abraham, have pity on me and send Lazarus to dip the tip of his finger in water and cool my tongue, because *I am in agony* in this fire."

But Abraham replied, "Son, remember that in your life-time you received your good things, while Lazarus received bad things, but now he is comforted here and you are in agony. And besides all this, between us and you a great chasm has been fixed, so that those who want to go from here to you cannot, nor can anyone cross over from there to us."

He answered, "Then I beg you, father, send Lazarus to my father's house, for I have five brothers. Let him warn them, so that they will not also come to *this place of torment*."

Abraham replied, "They have Moses and the Prophets; let them listen to them."

"No, father Abraham," he said, "but if someone from the dead goes to them, they will repent."

He said to him, "If they do not listen to Moses and the Prophets, they will not be convinced even if someone rises from the dead."

Can you even imagine what it was like? The rich man was in torment. He was in agony. He was far from heaven and would never get there. His situation was hopeless. He would never get out of that place of torment. He begged for a drop of water but did not receive it.

Even there, he did not learn his lesson. He did not accept God's will. He thought he knew better than God how his brothers should be approached and converted. He still had a low opinion of God's Word ("Moses and the Prophets"). Even if he had learned his lesson, it was far too late.

Deprivation

Hell is a place of deprivation. There the damned are deprived of every good thing. Pause to think of every good thing in life. Now realize that the occupants of hell have nothing good. There is no cold drink. There is no easy chair or comfortable place. There is no vacation. There is not even a break for a little relief. There is nothing good there. The residents of hell are deprived of everything that makes life enjoyable.

We could not even begin to list all of the things the damned will lack forever. There is no joy or happiness there. There is no hope for the future—no hope of getting out, of going back to earth, or of going to heaven. There is no chance of peace with God now. There is no opportunity for fellowship with the believers in heaven. There is an eternal separation. There is no pity or mercy either. The rich man received no pity. He did not receive one drop of water. There is no rest and no relief for the wicked in hell.

Wrath and anger

Hell is the ultimate expression of God's just punishment for sin. Selfish sinners may not realize what is waiting for them. People might think that it's no big deal to reject the gospel. Romans 2:8,9 reveals the future for unbelievers: "For those who are self-seeking and who reject the truth and follow evil, there will be wrath and anger. There will be trouble and distress for every human being who does evil." It is no picnic to suffer the wrath of God. We cannot even comprehend what this will really be like. It will certainly mean "trouble and distress." For good reason, Scripture says, "It is a dreadful thing to fall into the hands of the living God" (Hebrews 10:31).

People will want it to end, but it won't. They will wish that they could "die" and end it all. But they won't be able to. There is no escape. There is no exit. There is no hope. Revelation 14:11 says, "The smoke of their torment rises for ever and ever. There is no rest day or night" for unbelievers.

Loathsome

Some people today live for fame and fortune. Some would give up everything to be beautiful. But fame and beauty are fleeting. Then what happens to people who lived only for this life? If beautiful movie stars go to hell, will they still be beautiful? Certainly not! We know that unbelievers will rise in the resurrection of the dead on judgment day. But Scripture never even hints that their bodies will be glorified. Instead, it says just the opposite about those who rebelled against God. "Their worm will not die, nor will their fire be quenched, and they will be loathsome to all mankind" (Isaiah 66:24). Jesus quoted these words as a description of hell (Mark 9:48). In the resurrection, the bodies of unbelievers will be hideous and ugly. They will be disgusting and loathsome. Think about dead, decaying bodies that have worms or maggots gnawing on them. Think about bodies horribly scarred by terrible fire. These are the pictures used by Isaiah for the torment of hell. Certainly unbelievers in hell will be loathsome.

We might wonder how their "worm" (the one that they justly deserve) can keep bothering them and never die. We wonder how their fire will never go out and yet never completely consume them so that they can die and find relief. There is never a time when the suffering finally stops. It just keeps going on and on forever. This is hell. It is no joke.

Darkness

The Bible describes hell as a place of deep darkness (Matthew 8:12; 22:13; 25:30). This is the opposite of the heavenly light. God will condemn the evil spirits and all unbelievers to remain outside of the well-lighted banquet hall of heaven. They will be outside, kept from enjoying God's heavenly blessings. False teachers will go into "blackest darkness," the most gloomy place imaginable (2 Peter 2:17; Jude 13). Hell is ready and waiting for them. The evil spirits are already being punished with this darkness as they await their final judgment on the Last Day (Jude 6).

Weeping and gnashing of teeth

One of the most common biblical descriptions of hell is that unbelievers "will be thrown outside, into the darkness, where there will be weeping and gnashing of teeth" (Matthew 8:12; see also 13:42,50; 22:13; 24:51; 25:30). Luke 13:28 says, "There will be weeping there, and gnashing of teeth, when you see Abraham, Isaac and Jacob and all the prophets in the kingdom of God, but you yourselves thrown out." These words are repeated so often, we should all know what they mean.

There will be weeping and wailing in hell. It is a place of eternal sorrow. There is no happiness there. The condemned occupants of hell suffer hopeless sadness forever. Their weeping is like no other. It is a weeping that finds no solace, no comfort, and no help. The damned have faced final rejection from God. They cannot look forward to some appeal or parole. There is no mercy. It's over for them. It's really over, forever! It is not hard to see why they are overwhelmed with grief and sadness.

They gnash their teeth, grind them together. They suffer intense pain. They experience indescribable anguish and torment. It hurts worse than anything ever known in this world. They grit and grind their teeth as they suffer. In their agony, they do not think pleasant thoughts of God. He has condemned them for all eternity to this place of torment. So, they grind (gnash) their teeth in seething rage and anger. They hate God! Their thoughts are not pure and right. They think of their distressing situation, their excruciating tortures, and their hopeless future. They think about this, for all eternity, with a fierce and gnawing hatred for God. They grit and grind their teeth, and on and on this continues—forever.

Second death

In the book of Revelation, Jesus speaks of a *second death*. He says, "He who overcomes will not be hurt at all by the second death" (Revelation 2:11). Believers will not experience the second death. This is not talking about physical, temporal, death (when the soul separates from the body). Jesus teaches that his believers who keep his Word "will never see death" (John 8:51). He is talking about eternal death.

The Jews misunderstood. They thought he was talking about temporal death. They said, "Now we know that you are demon-possessed! Abraham died and so did the prophets, yet you say that if anyone keeps your word, he will never taste death" (verse 52). But Jesus was talking about the second death.

Revelation 20:6 reveals that the second death has no power over believers. Then verse 14 indicates that "the lake of fire is the second death." In other words, the second death is eternal death (separation from God) in hell. Remember that death means separation, not ceasing to exist. Unbelievers suffer this second death. "The cowardly, the unbelieving, the vile, the murderers, the sexually immoral, those who practice magic arts, the idolaters and all liars—their place will be in the fiery lake of burning sulfur. This is the second death" (Revelation 21:8). So, the second death is the eternal torment of hell. It is eternal separation from God's eternal blessings.

Destruction

Jesus says, "Enter through the narrow gate. For wide is the gate and broad is the road that leads to destruction, and many enter through it" (Matthew 7:13). Here, our Savior describes hell as destruction. But what does that mean? When the Bible describes hell as destruction, it is not talking about annihilation.

Second Thessalonians 1:9 says, "They will be punished with *everlasting destruction* and shut out from the presence of the Lord and from the majesty of his power." Everlasting destruction is destruction that lasts forever. It never ends. Although it is hard to understand this, the destruction of hell is a never-ending process that goes on and on for all eternity. It is like an everlasting process of decay. Jesus was quoting from Isaiah 66:24 when he described hell as a place where "their worm does not die, and the fire is not quenched" (Mark 9:48). Hell is a place of nonstop destruction and decay.

Degrees of punishment

Will there be different degrees of punishment in hell, or will everyone suffer the same punishment? Certainly, all of the suffering of hell is terrible. We would not want to have any part of it, even for a short time. But Scripture does teach that there will be different degrees of punishment.

Sodom and Gomorrah were exceedingly wicked (see Genesis 18:20–19:26). We don't have to wonder about what God thought of them. "They serve as an example of those who suffer the punishment of eternal fire" (Jude 7). But consider these words Jesus spoke to his twelve disciples before sending them out to do mission work among the lost sheep of Israel: "If anyone will not welcome you or listen to your words, shake the dust off your feet when you leave that home or town. I tell you the truth, it will be more bearable for Sodom and Gomorrah on the day of judgment than for that town" (Matthew 10:14,15).

If people would not welcome his disciples or listen to their words, it would be even worse for them than it would be for Sodom and Gomorrah! Sodom will certainly not have it good, but people who maliciously reject the gospel will have it even worse. Clearly, God takes his Word seriously. When people reject God's Word and his servants, they reject him and commit the most terrible crime. They will be punished most severely.

When our Lord Jesus repeats a teaching, we should take special notice. All of God's Word is important, but if our Savior takes the time to repeat a warning, we should take it most seriously. Read what Jesus says in Matthew 11:20-24:

> Then Jesus began to denounce the cities in which most of his miracles had been performed, because they did not repent. "Woe to you, Korazin! Woe to you, Bethsaida! If the miracles that were performed in you had been performed in Tyre and Sidon, they would have repented long ago in sackcloth and ashes. But I tell you, it will be more bearable for Tyre and Sidon on the day of judgment than for you. And you, Capernaum, will you be lifted up to the skies? No, you will go down to the depths. If the miracles that were performed in you had been performed in Sodom,

it would have remained to this day. But I tell you that it will be more bearable for Sodom on the day of judgment than for you."

Jesus says that it would be more bearable even for the wicked people of Sodom than it would be for those who reject Jesus and his Word. The people of Korazin and Bethsaida and the people of Capernaum had far greater opportunities to hear Jesus and repent. But they had rejected him, so they would suffer the worst punishment.

It is a terrible sin to reject the gospel message of salvation when it is proclaimed. Think of all the people who learn God's Word as children, perhaps from their parents or in Sunday school, and then reject it later in life. They know better. They have every opportunity. But they reject their Savior. The worst suffering of hell awaits them. Jesus says:

> "That servant who *knows* his master's will and does not get ready or does not do what his master wants will be beaten with *many* blows. But the one who *does not know* and does things deserving punishment will be beaten with *few* blows. From everyone who has been given much, much will be demanded; and from the one who has been entrusted with much, much more will be asked." (Luke 12:47,48)

God will take into account how many opportunities people had to hear his Word. God will consider what people knew. Those who had more opportunities and rejected them will be punished more severely. Those who knew more of God's Word and ignored it will be punished most terribly.

Romans 2:12 teaches the same truth: "All who sin apart from the law will also perish apart from the law, and all who sin under the law will be judged by the law." Gentiles and others who never heard the gospel will perish without an excuse (Romans 2:1). But the Jews and others who heard God's saving message and had God's Word will be judged by what was available to them. They had God's Word. They heard the gospel promise of the Savior from sin. Their punishment will be worse. The most severe punishment is reserved for those people who maliciously and purposely reject the gospel of Christ when it is brought to them.

Just think how such people will feel in hell. They will know that they had every opportunity to believe and go to heaven, but they rejected the gospel. They will have guilty consciences. They will know that they could have been in heaven. This thought will torture them for all eternity. Their suffering will be the worst. May we never find out by experience just how bad the suffering of hell really is.

> A book is opened then to all,
> A record truly telling
> What each has done, both great and small,
> When he on earth was dwelling,
> And ev'ry heart be clearly seen,
> And all be known as they have been
> In thoughts and words and actions.
>
> Then woe to those who scorned the Lord
> And sought but carnal pleasures,
> Who here despised his precious Word
> And loved their earthly treasures!
> With shame and trembling they will stand
> And at the judge's stern command
> To Satan be delivered.

My Savior paid the debt I owe
And for my sin was smitten;
Within the Book of Life I know
My name has now been written.
I will not doubt, for I am free,
And Satan cannot threaten me;
There is no condemnation! (CW 207:3-5)

6

Eternal Punishment

In Dante's description of hell, these words were above hell's gate: "Leave every hope, ye who enter!"[36] His imagination matches reality, because Scripture teaches that there is no hope in hell. There is no hope of relief. There is no hope of appeal. There is no hope that the suffering of hell will end.

Many false teachers (including Jehovah's Witnesses, Seventh-day Adventists, atheists, and a great number of liberal pastors and theologians) claim that there cannot be eternal punishment. Human reason argues that hell is too awful to last forever. It seems incomprehensible that there would be a punishment without end. So, people invent other explanations of hell.

Some false teachers try to explain hell as something that occurs in this world. They explain hell as the mess people make of their own lives. They suppose that such people suffer a hell on earth for their own mistakes. One author put it this way: "Today Christian theologians and preachers usually speak of hell symbolically as a this-world reality. Today hell is described as the mess—either individual or social—that men make out of this life. . . . A battlefield, a prison cell, a hate-filled marriage, or a broken friendship is Hell."[37]

But we must ask, Is that what the Bible really says? In the account of the rich man and poor Lazarus, the rich man did not begin to suffer the torment of hell until he died (Luke 16:19-26). His body was buried, and his soul went to hell. He could not return to this life.

Hell is the result of God's condemnation. Hebrews 9:27 insists that God judges each person at death. "Man is destined to die once, and *after that* to face judgment." So, God does not send people to hell while they are living in this world. They might be on the road to hell. They might be under God's wrath. But technically, they are not yet in hell.

Even among relatively conservative Christians, there are some who do not teach that hell is eternal punishment. Some Evangelical scholars teach that hell is annihilation, the end of existence. One wrote in the magazine *Christianity Today* that "God does not raise the wicked in order to torture them consciously forever, but rather to declare his judgment upon the wicked and to condemn them to extinction."[38]

But again, we must ask, Is that what the Bible really says? No, it doesn't. These scholars are trying to pass off their own false ideas as God's truth. God's Word is very clear in teaching that the punishment of hell lasts forever.

The punishment of hell lasts forever

In the Old Testament, we read that unbelievers will rise from death on the Last Day and be condemned to "shame and everlasting contempt" (Daniel 12:2). In the New Testament, Jesus reveals what he will say to the unbelievers on judgment day: "Depart from me, you who are cursed, into the eternal fire prepared for the devil and his angels" (Matthew 25:41). Notice very carefully that he says "*eternal* fire."

That is why Jesus warns people so seriously about sin. He says, "If your hand or your foot causes you to sin, cut it off and throw it away. It is better for you to enter life maimed or crippled than to have two hands or two feet and be thrown into eternal fire" (Matthew 18:8). There is no doubt what Jesus means with the words "eternal fire." In Mark 9:43, Jesus describes hell as a place where "the fire never goes out." Eternal fire *never* goes out. It has no end.

The New Testament epistles also describe hell this way. It is not a temporary punishment. It lasts forever. Our increasingly wicked society should wake up and take this warning to heart. Jude 7 says, "Sodom and Gomorrah and the surrounding towns gave themselves up to sexual immorality and perversion. They serve as an example of those who suffer the punishment of eternal fire." That same epistle says that hell is reserved for the wicked "forever" (verse 13). Unbelievers will be punished with "everlasting destruction" (2 Thessalonians 1:9).

Without a doubt, hell is eternal, everlasting, never-ending punishment. This is just as certain as the fact that believers will receive eternal, everlasting, never-ending life in heaven. These truths are taught side by side in the Scriptures. The unbelievers will be in hell for as long as the believers will be in heaven: forever. Jesus summarizes his judgment on the Last Day, "Then they [unbelievers] will go away to eternal punishment, but the righteous [believers] to eternal life" (Matthew 25:46).

God won't change his mind

The predicament of the unbelievers seems so hopeless that some imagine that maybe God will change his mind, perhaps sometime in the future. Malachi 3:6 does not hold out any hope of that happening. It records this message from God, "I the LORD do not change."

If God would change his mind, unbelievers would not actually receive eternal punishment. God would be guilty of lying because he said they would receive eternal punishment. Would God ever lie or change his mind? We find a clear answer from a faithful prophet of God in 1 Samuel 15:29. "He who is the Glory of Israel does not lie or change his mind; for he is not a man, that he should change his mind." (See also Numbers 23:19; Psalm 110:4; Jeremiah 4:28; and Titus 1:2.)

God never lies. He keeps his word. God has said with an oath, "They shall *never* enter my rest" (Psalm 95:11). Make no mistake about it. These people will *never* enter the rest of heaven. God was talking about unbelievers who perish (see Hebrews 3:11-19).

This life is our time of grace. This life is our only time to be brought to faith by God's own power working through his saving Word. This will take a miracle. And we dare not approach God with arrogance. Jesus says, "I tell you the truth, anyone who will not receive the kingdom of God like a little child will never enter it" (Mark 10:15). We do not need more of human reason. We need God's Word and the gift of faith. Remember what the Scripture says about where faith originates. God creates faith, but "faith comes from hearing the message, and the message is heard through the word of Christ" (Romans 10:17).

God's Word is the one thing in this life that we truly need (Luke 10:38-42). There is still time. Scripture says:

> Therefore, since the promise of entering his rest still stands, let us be careful that none of you be found to have fallen short of it. For we also have had the gospel preached to us, just as they did; but the message they heard was of no value to them, because those who heard did not combine it with faith. Now we who have believed enter that rest, just as God has said, "So I declared on oath in my anger, 'They shall never enter my rest.'" . . . And again in the passage above he says, "They shall never enter my rest."
>
> It still remains that some will enter that rest, and those who formerly had the gospel preached to them did not go in, because of their disobedience. Therefore God again set a certain day, calling it Today, when a long time later he spoke through David, as was said before: "Today, if you hear his voice, do not harden your hearts." (Hebrews 4:1-7)

When should we be serious about hearing God's saving Word? Today! When should we be serious about teaching God's Word to our children and grandchildren? Today! When should we be serious about reaching out to others with the only saving gospel? Today! May we tell everyone that though we are sinners, Jesus has paid for every sin with his death on the cross. "Believe in the Lord Jesus, and you will be saved" (Acts 16:31).

The worst part about hell

Everything about hell is bad. It is difficult to even contemplate how awful the suffering of hell really is and will be. May none of us ever find out from experience how bad it really is! But, the worst part about hell seems to be that it never ends. There are many terrible aspects to the suffering, but if there were an end to it, it would not be nearly as bad. The worst part about hell is that there is no exit—ever!

There is no way out and no end to the suffering. In hell, "the fire never goes out" and "their worm does not die, and the fire is not quenched" (Mark 9:43,48). Abraham explained to the condemned rich man, "Between us and you a great chasm has been fixed, so that those who want to go from here to you cannot, nor can anyone cross over from there to us" (Luke 16:26).

It is certainly true that those in hell will not get out until they have paid everything that they owe (Matthew 5:26). But they can't pay what they owe. Psalm 49:8 says, "The ransom for a life is costly, no payment is ever enough."

Of course, Jesus paid enough for all sinners when he died on the cross. John the Baptist said, "Whoever believes in the Son has eternal life, but whoever rejects the Son will not see life, for God's wrath remains on him" (John 3:36). God's wrath remains on all who do not believe in Jesus Christ as their Savior, and they will remain in hell for ever and ever.

There is no exit from hell—ever! Eternal punishment means never-ending punishment. This is punishment, not discipline or correction. Once a person is there, it is too late.

But surely, human reason argues, there must be breaks to this suffering. There must be times of brief relief. Workers are allowed breaks. Surely, the mind continues, there must be some breaks in hell, so people can have some relief from the excruciating sufferings of hell! But there are none. When the condemned rich man said, "Have pity on me," he received no pity. When he asked for a drop of water to cool his tongue, he received nothing (Luke 16:24-26). He was no longer rich to say the least.

The fire and torment of hell will go on and on and on. "It will not be quenched night and day; its smoke will rise forever" (Isaiah 34:10; see also 66:24). It is horrible even to think about this! Yet unbelievers must suffer this for all eternity. "The smoke of their torment rises for ever and ever. There is no rest day or night [for the unbelievers]" (Revelation 14:11). They will be the companions of their leader, the devil. Scripture says, "The devil, who deceived them, was thrown into the lake of burning sulfur. . . . [He and those with him] will be tormented day and night for ever and ever" (20:10).

Why has God revealed this doctrine in Scripture?

The doctrine of eternal punishment in hell is so horrible, some might wonder why God even reveals this doctrine in the Bible. The simple answer is that God wants everyone to be warned about hell. God doesn't want anyone to perish in hell. He wants everyone to repent (2 Peter 3:9). God "wants all men to be saved and to come to a knowledge of the truth" (1 Timothy 2:4).

John the Baptist warned the people of his day to repent before it was too late:

> When he saw many of the Pharisees and Sadducees coming to where he was baptizing, he said to them: "You brood of vipers! Who warned you to flee from the coming wrath? Produce fruit in keeping with repentance. And do not think you can say to yourselves, 'We have Abraham as our father.' I tell you that out of these stones God can raise up children for Abraham. The ax is already at the root of the

> trees, and every tree that does not produce good fruit will
> be cut down and thrown into the fire.
>
> "I baptize you with water for repentance. But after me will
> come one who is more powerful than I, whose sandals I
> am not fit to carry. He will baptize you with the Holy
> Spirit and with fire. His winnowing fork is in his hand,
> and he will clear his threshing floor, gathering his wheat
> into the barn and burning up the chaff with unquenchable
> fire." (Matthew 3:7-12)

John pointed forward to the coming of the Savior from
sin, Jesus Christ, the Lamb of God, who has taken away
the sin of the world. In his earthly ministry, Jesus also
warned people about hell. But he revealed that many
would not receive this warning with repentance and faith.
They would persecute and kill his called servants who
tried to warn them.

> How will you escape being condemned to hell? There-
> fore I am sending you prophets and wise men and teach-
> ers. Some of them you will kill and crucify; others you
> will flog in your synagogues and pursue from town to
> town. And so upon you will come all the righteous
> blood that has been shed on earth, from the blood of
> righteous Abel to the blood of Zechariah son of
> Berekiah, whom you murdered between the temple and
> the altar. (Matthew 23:33-35)

Whose fault is it when the wicked are condemned to eternal punishment?

God is perfect. He never deserves any blame. When
sinners are condemned, it is their own fault. Certainly,
the devil and the evil angels have their roles and deserve
blame. False teachers who mislead people have their roles
too and deserve blame. The wicked world deserves blame

too. But, ultimately, it is the fault of the sinners themselves. Jesus said, "O Jerusalem, Jerusalem, you who kill the prophets and stone those sent to you, how often I have longed to gather your children together, as a hen gathers her chicks under her wings, but you were not willing" (Matthew 23:37). Jesus wants to gather all sinners, but they won't have him.

"The Lord . . . is patient with you, not wanting anyone to perish, but everyone to come to repentance" (2 Peter 3:9). God "wants all men to be saved and to come to a knowledge of the truth" (1 Timothy 2:4). He wants everyone to believe in Jesus and receive eternal life.

When unbelievers are finally condemned, it is their own fault. They have rejected the salvation that Jesus freely provided for them. Then, the punishment will never end.

Genuine Lutherans believe what the Bible says. The Augsburg Confession summarizes the teaching of Scripture. It states that on the Last Day our Lord Jesus Christ will "condemn ungodly men and the devil to hell and eternal punishment." It rejects the teaching "that the devil and condemned men will not suffer eternal pain and torment."[39]

Teaching that the punishment of hell lasts forever is a sharp teaching of the law. Yet, it is a part of God's Word. The punishment of hell is everlasting. This is what genuine Lutherans believe, teach, and confess on the basis of God's Holy Word.

> God's Word is our great heritage
> And shall be ours forever;
> To spread its light from age to age
> Shall be our chief endeavor.
> Through life it guides our way;

In death it is our stay.
Lord, grant, while worlds endure,
We keep its teachings pure
Throughout all generations. (CW 293)

7

Hell Is Real

Have you ever heard someone tell a joke about going to hell? Some half seriously say that they know that they will be going there. They plan to have all the fun they can now. They laugh about it. Hearing people talk this way tends to trouble Christians and rightfully so. Hell is real. It is no joke!

Many so-called theologians deny the existence of hell. Some of them have even worn the label "Lutheran." Often, they fall into blasphemy when they claim that a loving God would never send anyone to hell. One so-called Lutheran professor denied the reality of hell when he wrote:

> That a just heavenly Father would condemn a child of
> his to burn in agony for all eternity, which is trillions and

trillions of years unending, because that child misused a mere seventy short years has always been appalling to many. . . . A heavenly Father who would fry his enemies to all eternity would seem to be infinitely worse than the monster Adolf Hitler who gassed and cremated at places like Buchenwald and Belsen some six million Jews whom he counted as his enemies. . . . Modern biblical scholars and theologians simply do not believe that Jesus said the things about Hell that are attributed to him in the Gospels, because these passages contradict everything that Jesus was and stood for. Jesus, for instance, exhorted us to love our enemies with a perfect—or complete— love such as the heavenly Father has. . . . Could this same Jesus really have agreed with the common opinion of his day that God overpunished his enemies after death with an everlasting grudge that roasted them in an eternal oven? No! I do not believe that Jesus would have agreed with that. For such a vengeful God, rather than being the marvelous deity of love and mercy and forgiveness, is in my eyes a Frankenstein of hatred and pitilessness and revenge who orders his children to be more moral than he is willing to be.[40]

Anyone who writes this way cannot be a genuine Lutheran. Real Lutherans don't deny clear Bible teachings. Jesus did say the things about hell that are attributed to him in the gospels, and genuine Lutherans agree with what he said. The Lutheran Confessions declare that at the end of the world "Christ will appear and raise all the dead, granting eternal life and eternal joys to the godly but condemning the ungodly to endless torment with the devil."[41] Yet, the "Lutheran" professor quoted above was not only denying the existence of hell, he was questioning God.

We have no right to question God! The Lord of heaven and earth could say to anyone what he said to

Job: "Who is this that darkens my counsel with words
without knowledge? Brace yourself like a man; I will
question you, and you shall answer me. Where were you
when I laid the earth's foundation? Tell me, if you understand" (Job 38:2-4).

We dare not trifle with God, "who alone is immortal
and who lives in unapproachable light, whom no one has
seen or can see. To him be honor and might forever"
(1 Timothy 6:16). God knows so much more than we do.
So, instead of questioning God, we should praise him for
his wisdom, with the words of Romans 11:33-36:

> Oh, the depth of the riches of the wisdom and knowledge
> of God! How unsearchable his judgments, and his paths
> beyond tracing out! "Who has known the mind of the
> Lord? Or who has been his counselor?" "Who has ever
> given to God, that God should repay him?" For from him
> and through him and to him are all things. To him be the
> glory forever! Amen.

Instead of questioning God, we should simply receive
his Word with thanksgiving and not doubt what he says
in Scripture.

We can be absolutely certain that there is a hell

It is strange that some of the very same people who
deny that there is a hell will still maintain that there is a
heaven. Yet, in Scripture, these two destinations are
often taught in the very same Bible passages. We can be
just as certain that there is a hell as we are that there is a
heaven. Or, to put it still another way: if there is a
heaven, then there is a hell. No one who follows the
Bible will say that there is a heaven but no hell. The
Bible teaches that both are real.

In Matthew 25:46, Jesus summarizes what will happen to unbelievers and believers on judgment day: "Then they [unbelievers] will go away to eternal punishment, but the righteous [believers] to eternal life." We can be certain that believers go to heaven. We can be just as certain that unbelievers go to hell. And hell is eternal punishment.

Many of us have memorized Mark 16:16, "Whoever believes and is baptized will be saved, but whoever does not believe will be condemned." Again, we see that it is certain that whoever believes will be saved in the final judgment. But, it is just as certain that whoever does not believe will be condemned. We can be absolutely certain that there is a hell and that unbelievers are going there.

Our certainty also rests on the fact that God never lies. "God is not a man, that he should lie, nor a son of man, that he should change his mind. Does he speak and then not act? Does he promise and not fulfill?" (Numbers 23:19). God has spoken. In the end, unbelievers will be condemned to eternal punishment. God does not lie. We can be sure that this will happen.

So, the matter is settled for a Bible believer. Hell is real. Unbelievers will suffer in a very real hell. But this is when some people appeal to human reason and human feelings of affection and ask, "How could a loving God send anyone to hell?" How would you answer that question? Again, let us search the Scriptures for the answer.

How can a loving God send anyone to hell?

It is true that God is loving. We do not deny that fact of Scripture. But, it is also true that God is just and holy. He punishes the wicked. Both of these statements are true. God is loving. God is just and punishes sinners. God reveals himself with his own name in Exodus 34:6,7:

"The LORD, the LORD, the compassionate and gracious God, slow to anger, abounding in love and faithfulness, maintaining love to thousands, and forgiving wickedness, rebellion and sin. *Yet he does not leave the guilty unpunished;* he punishes the children and their children for the sin of the fathers to the third and fourth generation."

Study these words carefully.

First, the Lord describes himself as "the compassionate and gracious God, slow to anger, abounding in love and faithfulness, maintaining love to thousands, and forgiving wickedness, rebellion and sin." This is the Lord we have come to know and love. We learn about him in the gospel. We love to hear of how he loved the whole world so much that he sent a Savior. We love to hear about how the Lord forgives all of our sins through Jesus.

But the passage does not stop there. Look again at the words in italic print, *"Yet he does not leave the guilty unpunished."* This is also true. We cannot and should not take a scissors and cut out the rest of this Bible passage. God is describing himself. He is a God of love; that is true. Yet he is also just. He punishes sin. That's why Jesus had to die on the cross. He received the punishment we deserved for our sins.

Either we had to receive eternal punishment for our sins or someone eternal had to die. Jesus, the eternal Son of God, was willing to die in our place. And that is how he won forgiveness for us. God did not just sweep our sins under the rug. There had to be punishment for sin, and Jesus received it in our place.

Make no mistake about it. God is just. "He is the Rock, his works are perfect, and all his ways are just. A faithful God who does no wrong, upright and *just* is he" (Deuteronomy 32:4). He does not leave the guilty unpunished. He has said, "The wages of sin is death" (Romans 6:23). So, anyone who rejects the payment Jesus made on the cross must suffer the just punishment for sin. Either the eternal Savior dies for you or you die for all eternity. Either you receive his payment on your behalf or you must pay what you owe forever in hell. That is a debt that is never paid off and lasts for all eternity.

Isn't it more loving to just not talk about hell?

I've heard it more than once. People don't want to hear about hell. They don't want to think about hell. So, we must consider this question: Is it more loving not to talk about hell?

It might seem like it, but it isn't. Suppose that you see a young couple enjoying some treats in a little boat as they slowly drift toward Niagara Falls. You know that they are moving closer and closer to the deadly waterfall. Yet they are enjoying themselves and having a nice afternoon. If you warn them, you will spoil their afternoon. They clearly do not wish to be bothered, and you are not inclined to bother them. On the other hand, they keep drifting. Which is more loving?

a. To politely say and do nothing as you let them enjoy their treats?

b. To lovingly warn them that they are in deep trouble because they are drifting toward a waterfall?

The first choice is not only easier for you, it seems so "loving." But it is not the right answer. It is not loving to simply let someone unknowingly drift toward destruction. In a similar way, if you know people who are living lives of unbelief and drifting toward eternal condemnation, the loving thing to do is to warn them. They might not want to be interrupted. They might not want to hear about hell. But warning them is the loving thing to do. Love moves us to warn people about hell so that we can tell them about Jesus, who redeemed all people from eternal punishment.

Besides, we cannot agree never to talk about hell because it is a clear Bible teaching. As a pastor, I have been called by God to preach and teach God's Word. When I was ordained and installed, I vowed to do this as a public minister of the gospel. The teaching about hell is a part of the Word of God. I have no right to simply delete that teaching from God's Word. Deuteronomy 4:2 says, "Do not add to what I command you and do not subtract from it, but keep the commands of the LORD your God that I give you." We have no right to subtract the teaching of hell from the Bible. But some false teachers are doing that very thing today.

Sometimes false teaching is not so much saying the wrong thing as not saying the right thing. It is just as false to subtract the teaching of hell as it is to add some false teaching like purgatory. Jesus says, "Watch out for false prophets. They come to you in sheep's clothing, but inwardly they are ferocious wolves" (Matthew 7:15).

Those who preach and teach God's Word must be faithful in communicating God's Word. The Lord has said, "Let the one who has my word speak it faithfully" (Jeremiah 23:28). Anyone who omits the teaching of everlasting punishment for unbelievers is certainly not a faithful teacher of God's Word. And the truth is that there are many who teach this way in pulpits today.

They are not alone. There are many church members who try to silence the teaching about hell. They don't want to hear it or talk about it. While we will admit that this sharp teaching of God's law is a difficult one, we must also insist that it is loving to teach it faithfully. Remember the illustration of the young couple in the boat that was drifting toward Niagara Falls. It is loving to warn people when they are in danger of perishing.

As if that were not enough, God does not leave this up to our discretion. We must warn people. In Ezekiel 33:6-8, the Lord says:

> "'If the watchman sees the sword coming and does not blow the trumpet to warn the people and the sword comes and takes the life of one of them, that man will be taken away because of his sin, but I will hold the watchman accountable for his blood.'

> "Son of man, I have made you a watchman for the house of Israel; so hear the word I speak and give them warning from me. When I say to the wicked, 'O wicked man, you will surely die,' and you do not speak out to dissuade him from his ways, that wicked man will die for his sin, and I will hold you accountable for his blood."

We do not want God to hold us accountable for others because we refused to warn them when they were living in a wicked way. If we warn them and they fail to listen, that's their own fault. But let's be sure to warn them! Maybe they will be moved to repent and we can declare them forgiven through Christ. May we have the mind of God when sinners stray.

> "As surely as I live," God said,
> "I would not have the sinner dead,
> But that he turn from error's ways,
> Repent, and live through endless days."

> To us, therefore, Christ gave command:
> "Go forth and preach in ev'ry land;

Bestow on all my pard'ning grace
Who will repent of sinful ways." (CW 308:1,2)

Jesus warned the wicked and called them to repent (see Matthew 4:17, for example). He commonly warned people that judgment day would come unexpectedly. "Therefore keep watch, because you do not know on what day your Lord will come" (Matthew 24:42). Jesus warned Judas Iscariot more than once. He warned the Pharisees and teachers of the law. The Lord patiently warns people, because he is "not wanting anyone to perish, but everyone to come to repentance" (2 Peter 3:9). Even though it is not a pleasant thought, Jesus goes so far as to say this as a loving warning:

> "If your hand causes you to sin, cut it off. It is better for you to enter life maimed than with two hands to go into hell, where the fire never goes out. And if your foot causes you to sin, cut it off. It is better for you to enter life crippled than to have two feet and be thrown into hell. And if your eye causes you to sin, pluck it out. It is better for you to enter the kingdom of God with one eye than to have two eyes and be thrown into hell, where 'their worm does not die, and the fire is not quenched.'" (Mark 9:43-48)

By this, Jesus is teaching self-mortification, not self-mutilation. We want to put our old Adam (sinful nature) to death so that we do not perish in sin. And yet the stark words are there. If I had to choose, I would rather lose a limb or an eye for this lifetime than end up in hell, wouldn't you? Now consider that pet temptation, and take it seriously. It is better to do without earthly pleasures than to forfeit your soul!

Our loving Lord warns us about the torments of hell so that we will not drift away from him. This is our time of grace. Our Lord wants us to make the most of it, by hearing his saving gospel and receiving the Lord's Supper. He wants us to grow in faith, as the Holy Spirit works in our hearts through Word and sacrament, so that we are ready when he returns. Read Matthew 25:1-13 for a lesson about the need for being ready by faith when Christ returns. On that Last Day, we will see that our Lord Jesus is both loving and just. He will be loving toward his believers as he graciously takes them to heaven. He will be just toward the unbelievers who rejected him. They will get what they justly deserve, forever.

So, we reach out and appeal to people with urgency, just as the apostle Paul did. "I tell you, now is the time of God's favor, now is the day of salvation" (2 Corinthians 6:2). Hear the gospel! Learn of Jesus! Tomorrow might be too late! Once a person is in hell, it is too late. It is only loving to tell people about God's Word now.

That's what the rich man in hell wanted to do (Luke 16:27,28). Maybe he had received plenty of warnings from God's Word and God's people in his lifetime. Maybe that's why he thought it would take a man who had risen from the dead to convince his brothers. He certainly would agree that the warning was necessary. That warning is found in the Bible ("Moses and the Prophets").

Whether people have many opportunities to hear the gospel or few, they will be judged. Even if people have never heard the gospel once, they will be judged. Anyone who does not believe in Jesus will be condemned to hell. They are, in the words of Scripture, "without excuse" (Romans 1:20). They should have known that God created the world. Anyone with sense knows that (Psalm 14:1). They should have sought out knowledge of God. Romans 1:20 says, "Since the creation of the world God's

invisible qualities—his eternal power and divine nature—
have been clearly seen, being understood from what has
been made, so that men are without excuse." There is no
excuse for being an atheist.

Will there be any atheists in hell?

This is more of a curious question than a practical one.
Certainly the devil and the evil angels (demons) know
that there is one God. "Even the demons believe that—
and shudder" (James 2:19). Isn't it rather fascinating to
know that not even the devil is an atheist? The condemned people in hell would have to know that there is a
God. After all, God is the one who condemns. All unbelievers will certainly see Jesus on judgment day. There will
be no atheists in hell. They will know that God exists. He
is their condemning judge.

What do we sinners deserve from God?

Let us never forget what we deserve from God. If God
would just give us what we deserve, we would receive eternal punishment.

> As it is written: "There is no one righteous, not even one;
> there is no one who understands, no one who seeks God.
> All have turned away, they have together become worth-
> less; there is no one who does good, not even one."
>
> Now we know that whatever the law says, it says to those
> who are under the law, so that every mouth may be
> silenced and the whole world held accountable to God.
>
> . . . for all have sinned and fall short of the glory of God.
> (Romans 3:10-12,19,23)

We all have sinned. We all deserve God's everlasting
wrath and punishment.

Yet, in spite of our sins, what has God done for us?

We do not deserve to have God love us. But he does love us. Jesus our Savior reveals that "God so loved the world that he gave his one and only Son, that whoever believes in him shall not perish but have eternal life" (John 3:16). God gave us the greatest gift. He gave us a Savior. Jesus Christ is our Savior. He rescued us from hell! He lived a perfect life and died on the cross to pay for all of our sins. Because he satisfied God's just demands, he rose from death on the third day. God has declared sinners "not guilty" and forgiven through Christ. Whoever believes in Jesus shall not perish in hell but will have everlasting life in heaven! In spite of our sins, God saved us!

Romans 6:23 puts it this way: "The wages of sin is death, but the gift of God is eternal life in Christ Jesus our Lord." What we deserve from God is everlasting punishment and eternal death. But what God has given us, through Christ, is everlasting life in heaven. Salvation is a free gift! Romans 5:6-9 explains all of this:

> You see, at just the right time, when we were still powerless, Christ died for the ungodly. Very rarely will anyone die for a righteous man, though for a good man someone might possibly dare to die. But God demonstrates his own love for us in this: While we were still sinners, Christ died for us.
>
> Since we have now been justified by his blood, how much more shall we be saved from God's wrath through him!

We have been justified, or acquitted, by the death of Jesus. By faith in Jesus, we will not have to face God's wrath. We believers will not have to perish in hell.

We can learn much about hell from Scripture, but let us thank God that we don't have to go there and learn more about it from experience! No matter how rough life seems to be, we can be thankful that we aren't in hell and we aren't going to be in hell forever! Now, isn't that a great reason to worship and praise our Savior? He rescued us from what we deserved.

8

The Bible's Definition of the Eternal Joys of Heaven

Sometimes the most difficult questions to answer come from little children. The tiniest tots ask questions like "Daddy, why is the sky blue?" "Mommy, where does the wind come from?" Just imagine if a child would tug on your coat and politely ask, "What is heaven?"

God wants us to be ready to answer questions. First Peter 3:15 says, "Always be prepared to give an answer to everyone who asks you to give the reason for the hope that you have." Are you ready to give the answer? What is heaven? There are many ways that we could answer that question. Let's search the Scriptures to see what the Bible teaches about heaven.

Eternal life

Old Testament believers could look forward to unending life with God in heaven. Daniel looked forward to judgment day and said, "Multitudes who sleep in the dust of the earth will awake: some to *everlasting life*, others to shame and everlasting contempt" (12:2). We live in the New Testament era. We have the same hope. John 3:16 says, "God so loved the world that he gave his one and only Son, that whoever believes in him shall not perish but have *eternal life*."

Not everyone receives this life. Jesus says, "Small is the gate and narrow the road that leads to *life*, and only a few find it" (Matthew 7:14). The problem is sin. Romans 6:23 tells us, "The wages of sin is death, but the gift of God is *eternal life* in Christ Jesus our Lord." We sinners deserve death (separation from God). But God gives us eternal life through Jesus Christ, who lived a perfect life for us and died on the cross as our substitute. He rose from death because he had won forgiveness for sinners. Jesus says, "I am the resurrection and the life. He who believes in me will *live*, even though he dies" (John 11:25). Heaven is eternal life after temporal death. It is the life believers live forever after this life has ended.

Salvation

God's Word describes heaven in terms of salvation, of being saved from eternal condemnation, and being saved in the final judgment. Jesus says, "Whoever believes and is baptized will be *saved*, but whoever does not believe will be condemned" (Mark 16:16). Later, the inspired apostle Paul wrote, "God did not appoint us to suffer wrath but to receive *salvation* through our Lord Jesus Christ" (1 Thessalonians 5:9).

Believers in Jesus are heirs of heaven. Believers "will inherit *salvation*" (Hebrews 1:14). They will finally be saved, body and soul, when Christ returns on the Last Day. Hebrews 9:28 explains that "Christ was sacrificed once to take away the sins of many people; and he will appear a second time, not to bear sin, but to bring *salvation* to those who are waiting for him."

Inheritance

Since we believers are heirs of heaven, Scripture describes heaven as our inheritance. On the Last Day, Jesus will say to his believers, "Come, you who are blessed by my Father; take your *inheritance*, the kingdom prepared for you since the creation of the world" (Matthew 25:34). Later, the inspired apostle Peter described heaven as "an *inheritance* that can never perish, spoil or fade" (1 Peter 1:4). Because the blood of Jesus Christ cleanses us from all sin and makes it possible for us to enter heaven, Hebrews 9:15 adds, "For this reason Christ is the mediator of a new covenant, that those who are called may receive the promised *eternal inheritance*—now that he has died as a ransom to set them free from the sins committed under the first covenant."

In the last book of the Bible, the Lord God delivers this clear promise to his believers: "He who overcomes will *inherit* all this, and I will be his God and he will be my son" (Revelation 21:7). If only we could see what we will inherit! Surely, heaven will be worth the wait. And, it will be worth any suffering that we must endure or overcome.

Glory

Scripture draws that comparison between our suffering and the great glory of heaven in Romans 8:17,18: "Now if we are children, then we are heirs—heirs of God and co-heirs with Christ, if indeed we share in his sufferings in order that we may also share in his *glory*. I consider that our present sufferings are not worth comparing with the *glory* that will be revealed in us." When compared to heaven, our suffering seems insignificant, "for our light and momentary troubles are achieving for us an *eternal glory* that far outweighs them all" (2 Corinthians 4:17). The apostle Paul strongly believed that heaven would be worth any amount of suffering that we might endure as Christians here.

Paul suffered because he brought the gospel to others as an apostle. In 2 Timothy 2:10, he revealed one key reason he was willing to put up with persecution and pain. "I endure everything for the sake of the elect, that they too may obtain the salvation that is in Christ Jesus, with *eternal glory*." The Bible describes heaven as eternal glory.

Rest

Scripture also describes heaven as a place of eternal rest. Revelation 14:13 says, "Blessed are the dead who die in the Lord from now on. Yes, . . . they will *rest* from their labor." This pleasant picture offers hope to believers who are tired and weary from the struggles of this life. The apostle Paul knew what it was like to become weary. Many called workers and laypeople in the church become weary too, serving the Lord under difficult conditions. Sometimes they can become discouraged and depressed, feeling unwanted, overstressed, and overworked. There is hope! We will rest forever in heaven. The more you suffer, the more tired and weary you become, the more appealing this description of heaven becomes.

Often God's people go without needed rest. They spend sleepless nights. They work hard. They suffer the cruel words and actions of unbelievers. But one day, God's people will rest in peace, basking in the perfect light of God's Son.

Those who oppose God and his message will not receive this rest. God has declared on oath in righteous anger, "They shall never enter my rest" (Psalm 95:11). We believers will enter that rest. Thanks be to God! Hebrews 4:9-11 encourages believers: "There remains, then, a *Sabbath-rest* for the people of God; for anyone who enters God's rest also rests from his own work, just as God did from his. Let us, therefore, make every effort to enter that *rest*."

Sometimes God's people die young. They die as children or in the prime of life. People ask, "Why?" Often, we do not know why God permits this to happen. But Isaiah 57:1,2 reveals that "the righteous are taken away to be spared from evil. Those who walk uprightly enter into peace; they find *rest* as they lie in death." Perhaps a child would have fallen into spiritual harm and temptation, so the Lord wisely and lovingly called the child home to be spared from evil. Perhaps a young person just needed to enter peace and rest early. God alone knows. But isn't it comforting to know that believers have it better in heaven than on earth? God's people truly do go to a better place! They find rest after death, thanks to Jesus.

I know of a sleep in Jesus' name,
A rest from all toil and sorrow;
Earth folds in her arms my weary frame
And shelters it till the morrow.
My soul is at home with God in heav'n;
My sorrows are past and over. (CW 211:1)

Wedding banquet/feast

One of the most common ways the Bible describes heaven is with the picture of a great feast. In Matthew 25:10, Jesus describes the heavenly feast as a wedding banquet: "But while they [foolish virgins] were on their way to buy the oil, the bridegroom arrived. The virgins who were ready went in with him to the *wedding banquet*. And the door was shut." Revelation 19:9 says, "Blessed are those who are invited to the *wedding supper* of the Lamb!" Those who are included in that heavenly banquet will be truly blessed and happy forever.

In parables, the heavenly banquet pictures the fellowship, pleasure, and joy we will have in the presence of our Savior in heaven. Heaven is too great for us to understand, so the Lord describes it in pictures. We must not insist on literally interpreting the details of these pictures. They are pictures to teach one main point. We will have joyful fellowship with our Savior in heaven.

Some of the Bible passages that speak of heaven as a feast appear in sections of Scripture that are not figurative. Jesus was talking about the great faith of the centurion when he said, "Many will come from the east and the west, and will take their places at *the feast* with Abraham, Isaac and Jacob in the kingdom of heaven" (Matthew 8:11). Jesus was speaking plainly to his disciples about the heavenly kingdom when he said, "You may eat and drink at my table in my kingdom" (Luke 22:30). When Jesus instituted the Sacrament of the Lord's Supper on Maundy Thursday, he said, "I tell you, I will not drink of this fruit of the vine from now on until that day when I drink it anew with you in my Father's kingdom" (Matthew 26:29). The "fruit of the vine" was wine. Will we drink wine in heaven in fellowship with Jesus?

Christ's words in the preceding paragraph support the idea that we will really eat and drink with Jesus in heaven, just as we really partake of the Lord's Supper here on earth. We know that we will have glorified bodies after judgment day. In the light of Christ's words quoted previously, I believe that we may enjoy good food and drink in a real feast in heaven. Yet we must be cautious about the specifics because "now we see but a poor reflection as in a mirror; then we shall see face to face. Now I know in part; then I shall know fully, even as I am fully known" (1 Corinthians 13:12).

Seeing God (vision of God)

Most Lutherans who write doctrine books about heaven state that the very essence of heaven is seeing God. The Old Testament believer Job looked forward to seeing God. He said, "After my skin has been destroyed, yet in my flesh I will *see* God; I myself will see him with my own eyes— I, and not another. How my heart yearns within me!" (Job 19:26,27). In the depth of his suffering, Job yearned to see God with his own eyes after the resurrection of the dead. Believers do well to look forward to seeing God. King David wrote, "And I—in righteousness I will *see your face*; when I awake, I will be satisfied with *seeing* your likeness" (Psalm 17:15). We will see God on judgment day. And we will be satisfied with seeing God. For all eternity, no matter how great the pleasures of heaven really are, nothing will give us greater satisfaction than seeing our Lord and Savior.

In the Beatitudes of his Sermon on the Mount, Jesus says, "Blessed are the pure in heart, for they will *see God*" (Matthew 5:8). Believers' sins are washed away, so their hearts are pure. Jesus says, "They will see God." The apostle Paul alluded to this face-to-face meeting when he wrote in

1 Corinthians 13:12, "Now we see but a poor reflection as in a mirror; then we shall see face to face." The author of the epistle to the Hebrews used this teaching to encourage sanctified living. "Make every effort to live in peace with all men and to be holy; without holiness no one will *see the Lord*" (12:14).

The apostle John wrote very clearly of this vision of God in 1 John 3:2: "Dear friends, now we are children of God, and what we will be has not yet been made known. But we know that when he appears, we shall be like him, for we shall *see him* as he is." We believers are the children of God. We will see God!

The last chapter of the Bible points us to the time when we will arrive safely in heaven and see our gracious God. The following description sounds a little like a return to the garden of Eden:

> Then the angel showed me the river of the water of life, as clear as crystal, flowing from the throne of God and of the Lamb down the middle of the great street of the city. On each side of the river stood *the tree of life*, bearing twelve crops of fruit, yielding its fruit every month. And the leaves of the tree are for the healing of the nations. No longer will there be any curse. The throne of God and of the Lamb will be in the city, and his servants will serve him. *They will see his face*, and his name will be on their foreheads. There will be no more night. They will not need the light of a lamp or the light of the sun, for the Lord God will give them light. And they will reign for ever and ever. (Revelation 22:1-5)

Others who see God

We believers are not the only ones who see God. The angels always see God too. Jesus says, "See that you do not look down on one of these little ones. For I tell you that their angels in heaven always *see the face of my Father* in heaven" (Matthew 18:10). Somehow it is possible for guardian angels always to see our heavenly Father's face while constantly protecting believers here. This is what leads some to say that heaven is not a place way out there somewhere. It could be like another dimension or realm that we simply are not allowed to see in this lifetime.

Not all who see Jesus returning on judgment day will be glad. Unbelievers will have good reason to be upset, afraid, and filled with sadness. Revelation 1:7 says, "Look, he is coming with the clouds, and every eye will see him, even those who pierced him; and all the peoples of the earth will mourn because of him. So shall it be! Amen." On the Last Day, "every eye will see" Jesus. All of the unbelievers will mourn for good reason. They will be condemned.

Believers do not mourn at the sight of our returning Savior. Believers have good reason to rejoice! Jesus says, "Now is your time of grief, but I will see you again and you will rejoice, and no one will take away your joy" (John 16:22). Believers will be saved in the final judgment and will enjoy the blessed view of God for all eternity.

So believers can even be glad in the midst of suffering. The apostle Peter was inspired to put it this way: "Rejoice that you participate in the sufferings of Christ, so that you may be overjoyed when his glory is revealed" (1 Peter 4:13). Jesus pictures this final meeting on judgment day as a joyous occasion for his believers. That's when Jesus will say, "Come and share your master's happiness!" (Matthew 25:23).

Let us praise "him who is able to keep you from falling and to present you before his glorious presence without fault and with great joy" (Jude 24). Let us praise him now and forever!

The home of God

"God is in heaven" (Psalm 115:3). Heaven is the home, or dwelling place, of God. Yet he is not confined to a certain location. "The LORD is God in heaven above and on the earth below" (Deuteronomy 4:39). God is present everywhere (omnipresent). King David realized this and asked, "Where can I go from your Spirit? Where can I flee from your presence? If I go up to the heavens, you are there; if I make my bed in the depths, you are there" (Psalm 139:7,8). So we must teach that God is everywhere and that God is in heaven. David was inspired to write, in another place, "The LORD has established his throne in heaven, and his kingdom rules over all" (Psalm 103:19). And again, we read in Psalm 115:3, "Our God is in heaven; he does whatever pleases him."

This leads sinners to great humility. Ecclesiastes 5:2 says, "Do not be quick with your mouth, do not be hasty in your heart to utter anything before God. God is in heaven and you are on earth, so let your words be few." God does hear. God has the power to judge and punish. According to God's law, there is good reason to be afraid of God. He is holy and we are sinners.

Yet the gospel tells another story. God lovingly sent our Savior. Through faith in Jesus, God is our loving Father. So we can pray "Our Father in heaven" as boldly and confidently as dear children speak to their dear fathers (Matthew 6:9). And our loving Father will answer our prayers. Jesus says, "If you then, though you are evil, know how to give good gifts to your children, how much more will your Father in heaven give the Holy Spirit to those who ask him!" (Luke 11:13).

Did you notice all three persons of the triune God in that sentence? Jesus is talking about his heavenly Father sending the Holy Spirit to his believers. All three persons of the triune God dwell in heaven. The one true God lives in heaven. After Jesus, the Son of God, redeemed us from sin, he ascended into heaven. Hebrews 1:3 puts it this way: "The Son is the radiance of God's glory and the exact representation of his being, sustaining all things by his powerful word. After he had provided purification for sins, he sat down at the right hand of the Majesty in heaven."

The home of angels

Heaven is the home of the angels too. Jesus is talking about his return on judgment day when he says, "No one knows about that day or hour, not even the angels in heaven" (Matthew 24:36). The angels are in heaven, living in eternal bliss. But even they do not know when Christ will return for the final judgment.

Jesus is talking again about the resurrection on that last day when he reveals that the angels live in heaven. He says, "When the dead rise, they will neither marry nor be given in marriage; they will be like the angels in heaven" (Mark 12:25). The angels in heaven do not marry.

The angels are very fast, but they are not present everywhere (omnipresent). Somehow, guardian angels see the Father in heaven. Jesus said, "See that you do not look down on one of these little ones. For I tell you that their angels in heaven always see the face of my Father in heaven" (Matthew 18:10).

The eternal home of believers

We're just strangers here. Heaven is our home. Heaven is the eternal home of everyone who believes in Jesus. When believing Lazarus died, his soul went to heaven. Revelation chapter 6 reveals that the souls of the faithful martyrs are in heaven right now. John later wrote, "I saw the souls of those who had been beheaded because of their testimony for Jesus and because of the word of God" (Revelation 20:4). Those souls are in heaven! The believers who have already died are God's "family in heaven" while we are God's family "on earth" (Ephesians 3:15). They are the church triumphant; we are the church militant.

On the Last Day, after the resurrection of the dead, Jesus will take all of us to heaven together, body and soul. Jesus "will say to those on his right, 'Come, you who are blessed by my Father; take your inheritance, the kingdom prepared for you since the creation of the world'" (Matthew 25:34). Then all his believers will enter eternal glory.

Heaven is the home of all who believe in Jesus. Of course, not all people are believers, and not all will enter heaven. Jesus warned unbelievers, "There will be weeping there, and gnashing of teeth, when you see Abraham, Isaac and Jacob and all the prophets in the kingdom of God, but you yourselves thrown out" (Luke 13:28). With these words, Jesus reveals the names of some souls already in heaven. Abraham, Isaac, and Jacob are in heaven. All the faithful prophets are in heaven. May we join them!

> I'm but a stranger here; Heav'n is my home.
> Earth is a desert drear; Heav'n is my home.
> Danger and sorrow stand Round me on ev'ry hand.
> Heav'n is my fatherland; Heav'n is my home.
>
> There at my Savior's side—Heav'n is my home—
> I shall be glorified; Heav'n is my home.
> There are the good and blest, Those I love most and best,
> And there I, too, shall rest; Heav'n is my home.
>
> (CW 417:1,3)

The way to heaven

How can we join the patriarchs and prophets? How can we be included in the number of those who are going to heaven? By now, you must have caught the answer, but just in case, let's review. Jesus says, "God so loved the world that he gave his one and only Son, that whoever believes in him shall not perish but have eternal life" (John 3:16). Jesus is God's Son. He lived a perfect life for us. He died on the cross in our place to pay our ransom. He rose from death. He won forgiveness for all people! Whoever believes in Jesus will receive eternal life. In another place, Jesus says, "Whoever believes and is baptized will be saved" (Mark 16:16). May God grant that to us all! May we all believe in Jesus and reach the magnificent eternal home God has prepared for us in heaven.

God is already there. The angels are already there. The departed believers are already there. May we arrive safely there too!

We began this chapter with the question of a child: "What is heaven?" Now what would you say to the child who asks that question? You might say something like this: "Heaven is where believers in Jesus go to enjoy life with God forever."

9

Heaven: Before and After Judgment Day

It's amazing what a computer Bible can do. I just ran a search of the word *heaven* in my computer version of the NIV. Instantly, 422 uses of this term appeared. Another 173 uses appeared when I typed in *heavens*. Clearly the term *heaven(s)* appears often in the Bible, too often to study every use in a book of this size. But, as you read through the long lists of Bible passages in which *heaven(s)* is used, it becomes clear that there are three main definitions.

Sky

The first use of *heaven(s)* is in the very first verse of the Bible. Genesis 1:1 says, "In the beginning God created the *heavens* and the earth." It seems difficult to nail down

exactly what *heavens* means here. Basically, the heavens
are what you see above you when you look up. This phrase
"the heavens and the earth" appears ten times in the Old
Testament. It seems to be a catchall term for the universe.
Exodus 20:11 has a slightly different expression when it
says, "In six days the LORD made the *heavens* and the
earth, the sea, and all that is in them." The term *heavens*
seems to be used for everything above us from our perspective on earth.

In Genesis 1:20 the NIV translates the Hebrew term for
heavens with the word *sky*. "God said, . . . 'Let birds fly above
the earth across *the expanse of the sky [heavens]*.'" Here,
heaven is the place where the birds fly above the earth.

Psalm 19:1 reveals through parallel phrases in Hebrew
poetry that *heaven* can indeed mean "sky." "The *heavens*
declare the glory of God; the *skies* proclaim the work
of his hands." Heavens and skies are the same thing in
this passage.

When I was a little boy, I misunderstood the intent of
those who built the tower of Babel. I thought they were
trying to build a building to heaven itself, but now I know
that they were trying to build a skyscraper, a building that
reached up to the skies. Their wickedness was in disobeying God's command to spread out all over the world. The
builders of the tower said, "Come, let us build ourselves a
city, with a tower that reaches to the *heavens*, so that we
may make a name for ourselves and not be scattered over
the face of the whole earth" (Genesis 11:4).

Outer space

Sometimes the term *heaven(s)* can mean outer space. In
Genesis 1:14-16, God says:

"Let there be lights in *the expanse of the sky* [heavens] to separate the day from the night, and let them serve as signs to mark seasons and days and years, and let them be lights in *the expanse of the sky* [heavens] to give light on the earth." And it was so. God made two great lights—the greater light to govern the day and the lesser light to govern the night. He also made the stars.

Once again, the heavens are what you see above you when you look up from the earth. When you look up during the day, you see the sun. When you look up at night, you see the moon and the stars. The sun, moon, and stars are in the expanse of the sky. They are in the heavens. They are in what we now call outer space.

When God was giving his great and gracious promises to Abraham, he took the man of faith outside and said, "Look up at the *heavens* and count the stars—if indeed you can count them." Then God said to Abraham, "So shall your offspring be" (Genesis 15:5). When God said, "Look up at the heavens," he was inviting Abraham to look to outer space, where the stars are. Perhaps this helps us understand Deuteronomy 10:14: "To the LORD your God belong the *heavens, even the highest heavens*, the earth and everything in it." Heaven can be the sky. It can be outer space. Or it can be what we commonly call heaven.

Heaven/paradise

Strictly speaking, heaven is the dwelling place of God. Psalm 115:3 says, "Our God is in heaven; he does whatever pleases him." Ecclesiastes 5:2 applies this truth: "Do not be quick with your mouth, do not be hasty in your heart to utter anything before God. God is in heaven and you are on earth, so let your words be few."

So, the first heaven is the sky. The second heaven is outer space. And the third heaven is, well, heaven! The apostle Paul calls heaven the third heaven in 2 Corinthians 12:1-4:

> I must go on boasting. Although there is nothing to be gained, I will go on to visions and revelations from the Lord. I know a man in Christ who fourteen years ago was *caught up to the third heaven*. Whether it was in the body or out of the body I do not know—God knows. And I know that this man—whether in the body or apart from the body I do not know, but God knows—was *caught up to paradise*. He heard inexpressible things, things that man is not permitted to tell.

The phrases in italics reveal that the third heaven is the same place as paradise. Paul was caught up to the third heaven, which is paradise. For the purposes of clarity in this book, we will reserve the use of the term *heaven*, as much as possible, for this third heaven, which is paradise.

The heavens	
first heaven	sky
second heaven	outer space
third heaven	heaven, or paradise

The location of heaven

Where is the third heaven, the place where God dwells? Most believers tend to think of heaven as somewhere up there, without thinking of any place in particular. Actually, there are Bible passages that lead us to think that way. When Jesus ascended, the Bible says, "He was taken up into heaven" (Mark 16:19). The disciples watched Jesus go upward, but where did he go? "A cloud hid him from their sight" (Acts 1:9). The disciples kept staring into the sky. Two angels explained that Jesus had been taken "into heaven" (verse 11).

There, Jesus sits "at the right hand of God" (Mark 16:19). He remains "seated at the right hand of God" (Colossians 3:1). When Stephen the martyr was dying, he "looked up to heaven and saw the glory of God, and Jesus standing at the right hand of God" (Acts 7:55). According to Hebrews 10:12, Jesus "sat down at the right hand of God" after he "had offered for all time one sacrifice for sins." As our Great High Priest, he is exalted and glorified in heaven.

We must ask, "What or where is the right hand of God?" Ephesians chapter 1 explains that since Jesus is seated at the right hand of God in heaven, he is "far above all rule and authority, power and dominion, and every title that can be given, not only in the present age but also in the one to come" (verse 21). The right hand of God is the ultimate position of authority. Jesus is above everyone else. "God placed all things under his feet and appointed him to be head over everything for the church" (verse 22). Jesus rules over the entire universe. He takes care of the invisible church of all true believers. He rules in the best interests of his believers. So, the right hand of God is a position of authority.

We should not think of it as a place somewhere "out there," because Ephesians chapter 4 tells us that Jesus "ascended higher than all the heavens, in order to fill the whole universe" (verse 10). Jesus ascended to the right hand of God so that he fills the whole universe. We must not think that Jesus is locally confined to a chair on the right side of God the Father. The triune God is omnipresent (present everywhere). Even if Jesus would be locally positioned just to the right side of God the Father, that still would put him everywhere.

Jesus Christ explains what sitting at the right hand of God the Father means when he says, "All authority in heaven and on earth has been given to me" (Matthew 28:18). He is at the position of authority. He is everywhere at once. Jesus says, "Surely I am with you always, to the very end of the age" (verse 20).

So Jesus is in heaven, and he is everywhere at once, all at the same time! In fact, Jesus was in heaven while he walked on this earth! As the second person of the triune God in the flesh, Jesus is in an intimate relationship with God the Father and God the Holy Spirit. As the God-man, Jesus was in heaven even while he was on earth. He revealed this when he spoke to Nicodemus. Jesus said, "No one has ever gone into heaven except the one who came from heaven—the Son of Man *who is in heaven*" (John 3:13). The NIV places the italicized phrase in a footnote, while the KJV and the NKJV leave it in the text. There is good evidence that these words should be included in the text. The problem is that many people cannot fathom how this could be possible. Jesus is true God! He can do the impossible, "for in Christ all the full-ness of the Deity lives in bodily form" (Colossians 2:9). In Jesus all the fullness of God was dwelling in bodily form! God is in heaven. Therefore, Jesus, being the God-man, was in heaven at the same time he was here on earth. This is rather deep, but why would we expect to fit all of the mysteries of the triune God into our tiny sin-poisoned human minds?

Scripture has more to say about where heaven is. Let's take a close look at the angels, those mighty spirits who serve believers. We know that angels are in heaven, right? And we know that the angels protect us. Psalm 91:11,12 says, "For he [God] will command his angels concerning you to guard you in all your ways; they will lift you up in their hands, so that you will not strike your foot against a stone." Angels are very, very fast, but they are not omnipresent. God can be everywhere at once. Angels can't. So, try to answer this question: Are the angels in heaven or on earth, or both?

Take a look at what Jesus says in Matthew 18:10: "See that you do not look down on one of these little ones. For I tell you that their angels in heaven always see the face of my Father in heaven." Did you catch that? The phrase "their angels" is talking about guardian angels. The angels who protect "these little ones," these believers, certainly must be on earth. These angels are guarding God's people. Yet, at the same time, these very same guardian angels are described as being in heaven. Further still, Jesus says that they "always see the face of my Father in heaven." How can they do that? They are not omnipresent. Yet they can guard God's people on earth and be in heaven seeing God all at the same time!

This is what led one very astute theology professor to say that heaven might be another dimension. After studying some of the same Bible passages we have just studied, Dr. Siegbert Becker wrote, "It is thus perhaps more in keeping with the words of the Bible to think of heaven not as a place far beyond the stars but simply as another realm of existence or another dimension of being."[42]

Heaven before judgment day

We have already learned that God is in heaven and the angels are in heaven. The souls of believers are in heaven too, but not their bodies. There are only a couple of very rare exceptions to this rule (Enoch and Elijah never died; see Genesis 5:24; Hebrews 11:5; and 2 Kings 2:11). Ecclesiastes 12:7 says, "The dust returns to the ground it came from, and the spirit returns to God who gave it." When Jesus said to the malefactor who believed, "Today you will be with me in paradise" (Luke 23:43), our Lord meant that what would go to heaven that very day was this man's soul, not his body.

Believers live on after this life. Their bodies are buried and decay. Sometimes their bodies are burned. But the souls of believers live on in heaven. When Jesus died, he committed his soul into his heavenly Father's hands (Luke 23:46). His soul went to heaven. That same day Jesus told the robber who had become a believer while hanging on a different cross, "I tell you the truth, today you will be with me in paradise" (verse 43). Jesus went to paradise when he died, and this ex-robber was with Jesus in paradise that same day. Stephen the martyr saw Jesus in heaven. Then, he prayed, "Lord Jesus, receive my spirit" (Acts 7:59). When faithful Stephen "fell asleep" in death (verse 60), his soul went straight to heaven.

We know for sure that Abraham is in heaven. Genesis 25:8 tells us that when that great man of faith died, "he was gathered to his people." His soul went to heaven. In the account of the rich man and poor Lazarus, Lazarus is in heaven with Abraham (Luke 16:22,25). Their souls are in heaven, not their bodies.

Believers can even look forward to dying, because they leave their bodies behind and go to heaven. The apostle

Paul was moved to write, "We are confident, I say, and would prefer to be away from the body and at home with the Lord" (2 Corinthians 5:8). Believers in Jesus may very well "desire to depart and be with Christ, which is better by far" (Philippians 1:23).

The apostle John was given a vision of heaven. God permitted him to see the *souls* of the martyrs in heaven. In Revelation 6:10, John wrote that the *souls* of the martyrs in heaven were wondering how long it would be until the Lord would judge the earth and avenge their blood. In chapter 20 of that same book, John wrote, "*I saw the souls* of those who had been beheaded because of their testimony for Jesus and because of the word of God" (verse 4).

Dr. Becker provides this helpful comment:

> When John says that he saw the souls of those who had been beheaded, it was just as though he were saying to a sorrowing church, "The government of the empire has beheaded our brothers and sisters in Christ. It seems that the enemies of the church have triumphed and the church is going down in defeat. Our friends are dead. But the government has only killed their bodies. And that is all we, too, see with these mortal eyes. But God granted me a vision in which I saw their souls. Those souls were not lying there on the bloody sand. They were sitting on thrones in heaven. They were not dead. They were living and reigning with Christ." What a message of encouragement and hope![43]

May we find encouragement and hope in these words of Scripture too.

Have you ever paused to wonder what it might be like to enter heaven? When you piece together all of the Bible passages, it is still hard to imagine what it will be like. This much we know: it will be wonderful and perfect and beyond our wildest dreams. It will give us great joy to finally see our Savior's face and be with him for all eternity. It will be great to join the other believers in heaven. But before judgment day, only our souls will be in heaven.

Judgment day

On judgment day, Jesus will raise all the dead. If we have died by that time, he will also raise our bodies from the grave. Our souls will be reunited with our bodies. Our bodies will be glorified. We believe what Scripture teaches about judgment day:

> We believe that Jesus died and rose again and so we believe that God will bring with Jesus those who have fallen asleep in him. According to the Lord's own word, we tell you that we who are still alive, who are left till the coming of the Lord, will certainly not precede those who have fallen asleep. For the Lord himself will come down from heaven, with a loud command, with the voice of the archangel and with the trumpet call of God, and the dead in Christ will rise first. After that, we who are still alive and are left will be caught up together with them in the clouds to meet the Lord in the air. And so we will be with the Lord forever. (1 Thessalonians 4:14-17)

The doctrinal pamphlet *This We Believe* explains:

> We believe that when Jesus returns and his voice is heard throughout the earth, all the dead will rise, that is, their souls will be reunited with their bodies (John 5:28,29). Together with those still living, the resurrected will appear before his throne of judgment. The unbelievers will be condemned to an eternity in hell. Those who by faith have been cleansed in the blood of Christ will be glorified and will live with Jesus forever in the blessed presence of God in heaven. (Philippians 3:21)[44]

Heaven after judgment day

After judgment day, each believer will be in heaven with body and soul. We will have our same bodies. The Old Testament believer Job eagerly looked forward to this. He said: "I know that my Redeemer lives, and that in the end he will stand upon the earth. And after my skin has been destroyed, yet in my flesh I will see God; I myself will see him with my own eyes—I, and not another. How my heart yearns within me!" (Job 19:25-27). Job knew that when he died, his body would decay. But, by faith, he also knew that he would rise from death. He knew that he would see God with his own eyes. He would experience the blessed vision of God for all eternity.

Jesus teaches that on the Last Day, "all who are in their graves will hear his voice and come out" (John 5:28,29). Jesus will raise all the dead. Martha, the sister of Lazarus, knew this. When her brother died, Martha took comfort in this fact. She said, "I know he will rise again in the resurrection at the last day" (11:24).

Resurrection body

The bodies of believers will rise from death. They will be glorified so that they no longer appear decayed and rotten. They will be perfect, like the body of our risen Savior. Philippians 3:20,21 says, "The Lord Jesus Christ . . . will transform our lowly bodies so that they will be like his glorious body." The Lord revealed to his Old Testament believers that "those who are wise *will shine* like the brightness of the heavens, and those who lead many to righteousness, *like the stars* for ever and ever" (Daniel 12:3). This sounds wonderful, but it is difficult for us to comprehend or explain. What will our bodies really be like?

One place to study for more information is the great resurrection chapter of the Bible: 1 Corinthians chapter 15. There we read: "So will it be with the resurrection of the dead. The body that is sown is perishable, it is raised imperishable; it is sown in dishonor, it is raised in glory; it is sown in weakness, it is raised in power; it is sown a natural body, it is raised a spiritual body" (verses 42-44).

When believers rise from death, they will have imperishable bodies. They will never die again. They will be raised in glory and in power. Every believer will have a spiritual body.

It is difficult to know what exactly is meant by "spiritual body." Usually spirits are invisible. But, it does not seem likely that we will be invisible, like spirits. We will have the same bodies, though glorified, that we had before we died. In the Old Testament, Job said, "In my flesh I will see God . . . with my own eyes—I, and not another" (Job 19:25-27).

Philippians 3:21 reveals that our Savior "will transform our lowly bodies so that they will be like his glorious body." Our bodies will be transformed, but they will be bodies like our risen Savior's glorious body. He was certainly no ghost. He proved this after he rose from death.

> "Look at my hands and my feet. It is I myself! Touch me and see; a ghost does not have flesh and bones, as you see I have."

> When he had said this, he showed them his hands and feet. And while they still did not believe it because of joy and amazement, he asked them, "Do you have anything here to eat?" They gave him a piece of broiled fish, and he took it and ate it in their presence. (Luke 24:39-43)

Our Savior's risen body had flesh and bones. His body was material. He even ate a piece of broiled fish. Our bodies will be like the body of our risen Savior. We will have flesh and bones too. Might this be a clue that we will be able to enjoy food in heaven? It seems likely, but we must wait until we arrive there to be sure.

Most likely, the term *spiritual* (1 Corinthians 15:44) refers to the exalted state of the risen bodies of believers. No longer will our bodies be subject to the effects or temptations of sin. No longer will we have to endure the negative work of our old Adam. Our bodies will be fully in tune with God's will, completely in step with the Holy Spirit. Now, we must struggle with the constant conflict between the old sinful nature and the new nature. When we rise from death, our bodies will be one hundred percent new nature and zero percent old sinful nature.

This much is certain: all of the dead will rise. For believers, then, death is only a sleep from which Jesus will awaken us. (See Matthew 9:24; John 11:11; and 1 Thessalonians 4:13.) When that happens, "the righteous *will shine like the sun* in the kingdom of their Father" (Matthew 13:43).

The new heavens and the new earth

Scripture describes the eternal home of believers as the new heavens and the new earth. This is heaven after judgment day. The Lord says, "Behold, I will create new heavens and a new earth. The former things will not be remembered, nor will they come to mind" (Isaiah 65:17). This home will endure forever (66:22). With faith in God's promise, "we are looking forward to a new heaven and a new earth, the home of righteousness" (2 Peter 3:13). This will be the home of all the righteous, all the believers whose sins were washed away and who were clothed with the righteousness of Jesus Christ. The apostle John looked ahead and saw our home. He wrote, "I saw a new heaven and a new earth, for the first heaven and the first earth had passed away" (Revelation 21:1). Soon, we believers will be with Jesus in our heavenly home. That is what our Lord promised when he said:

> "Do not let your hearts be troubled. Trust in God; trust also in me. In my Father's house are many rooms; if it were not so, I would have told you. I am going to prepare a place for you. And if I go and prepare a place for you, I will come back and take you to be with me that you also may be where I am. You know the way to the place where I am going. . . . I am the way and the truth and the life. No one comes to the Father except through me." (John 14:1-6)

Annihilation or renovation?

When the universe is destroyed on judgment day, will all matter and material be annihilated or will it be destroyed so that it can be renovated? Most Christians simply assume that when the Bible speaks of the world being destroyed it means annihilation, that nothing at all will remain. At first reading, this selection from 2 Peter 3:6-13 seems to sound that way. But, as you study these words, note carefully how the term *destroyed* is used.

> By these waters also the world of that time was deluged and *destroyed*. By the same word the present heavens and earth are reserved for fire, being kept for the day of judgment and destruction of ungodly men.

> But do not forget this one thing, dear friends: With the Lord a day is like a thousand years, and a thousand years are like a day. The Lord is not slow in keeping his promise, as some understand slowness. He is patient with

you, not wanting anyone to perish, but everyone to come to repentance.

But the day of the Lord will come like a thief. The heavens will disappear with a roar; the elements will be *destroyed* by fire, and the earth and everything in it will be laid bare.

Since everything will be destroyed in this way, what kind of people ought you to be? You ought to live holy and godly lives as you look forward to the day of God and speed its coming. That day will bring about the *destruction* of the heavens by fire, and the elements will *melt* in the heat. But in keeping with his promise we are looking forward to a *new heaven and a new earth*, the home of righteousness.

The world was flooded and destroyed at the time of Noah. At the end of the world, our present world will be destroyed too. But the flood did not annihilate the world in such a way that nothing at all was left. Could it be that after the elements are destroyed by fire, God will create the new heavens and the new earth from the material left after the destruction of the world? Destruction by fire does not necessarily mean that all matter disappears. The Bible uses the same word *destruction* to describe what happened in the worldwide flood and what will happen at the end of the world (by fire). Might there be material remaining?

Romans 8:18-23 also seems to allow for that understanding. There the inspired apostle wrote that the present creation is waiting to be liberated from the effects and consequences of sin. As you study these words, try to answer the previous question. Will the creation cease to exist, or will it be destroyed and renovated?

I consider that our present sufferings are not worth comparing with the glory that will be revealed in us. *The creation waits* in eager expectation for the sons of God to be revealed. For the creation was subjected to frustration, not by its own choice, but by the will of the one who subjected it, in hope that *the creation itself will be liberated* from its bondage to decay and brought into the glorious freedom of the children of God.

We know that the whole creation has been groaning as in the pains of childbirth right up to the present time. Not only so, but we ourselves, who have the firstfruits of the Spirit, groan inwardly as we wait eagerly for our adoption as sons, the redemption of our bodies.

Creation itself is going to be liberated, set free, from its bondage to decay. Creation itself is going to be free from those terrible effects of sin. Ever since sin entered the world, this world has not been right. There are environmental problems and natural disasters. There are scars all over the world. "*The creation itself* will be *liberated*." What does that mean?

Some believe this means that God will destroy the whole universe with fire, melt everything down, and then reuse that material to make a new heaven and a new earth when "the time comes for God to restore everything, as he promised long ago through his holy prophets" (Acts 3:21). That could be what these words mean. But we should be cautious about asserting this as a certainty. We are certain only that the whole world will be destroyed on the Last Day with fire.

Thank God, we will be kept safe with Jesus! He will return on the Last Day and raise all the dead. After the believers have risen from death, "we who are still alive and are left will be caught up together with them in the clouds to meet the Lord in the air. And so we will be with the Lord forever" (1 Thessalonians 4:17).

Forever with the Lord!
Amen! So let it be.
Life from the dead is in that word,
My immortality.

I'll know as I am known;
How shall I love that word
And oft repeat before the throne,
"Forever with the Lord!" (CW 213:1,6)

10

The Bible's Description of Heaven

Eternal life in heaven is even better than we can imagine. Life in heaven is so great, we cannot possibly comprehend it while we live in this sin-ruined world. We know what it is like to live in a sinful world. We do not really know what it is like to live in a world that is perfect and holy. The Bible commonly describes heaven by revealing that it will not be like this sinful world. The Holy Spirit uses what we know to explain what we do not know. Heaven will not be like the world that we know so well. Heaven will be very different.

When believers get to heaven, God "will wipe every tear from their eyes. There will be no more death or mourning or crying or pain, for the old order of things has passed away" (Revelation 21:4). The "old order of things" is this sinful world. When we get to heaven, this sinful world, with all of its problems and pains, will be behind us.

Rest assured, dear believers, God will answer our petitions that he deliver us from evil. When God takes us to heaven, he will be delivering us from every evil attack. Near the end of his life, the apostle Paul was inspired to write, "The Lord will rescue me from every evil attack and will bring me safely to his heavenly kingdom" (2 Timothy 4:18). This world is full of evil attacks on our faith. The devil, this world, and our own sinful flesh work against God's good purposes for us. But when we get to heaven, we will be free from these evil attacks.

And we will be free from death too. In fact, "The last enemy to be destroyed is death" (1 Corinthians 15:26). When we arrive safely in heaven, we will be immortal. People have searched all over this world trying to find a "fountain of youth," but there is none to be found. Even if there were, this world would remain full of pain and suffering. Who would want to stay here forever? But heaven is perfect. When we arrive there, we will never die again (verses 54-57).

Look forward to heaven!

We believers have good reason to look forward to our heavenly home. As our Lord has said, in this world, we have "trouble" (John 16:33). But "God is just: He will pay back trouble to those who trouble you and give relief to you who are troubled" (2 Thessalonians 1:6,7). Think of all the troubles believers have faced in this life simply because they confessed their faith in Jesus Christ as their Savior. Some became martyrs. Some lost their freedom. Some lost the respect of others. Some lost friends. Some faced ridicule. By faith in Christ, all of these believers go to heaven. When they get to heaven, their troubles and tribulations are left behind them. When they get to heaven, these believers have finally "come out of the great tribulation" (Revelation 7:14). If you have suffered for being a Christian, you know heaven is something to look forward to!

Some people are afraid of judgment day. But we believers have nothing to fear. Our Savior is returning to take us out of this world of trouble. He is going to take us home to heaven. So, when you see the events of judgment day happen, "stand up and lift up your heads, because your redemption is drawing near" (Luke 21:28). Your final redemption has arrived!

What have you suffered simply because you are a Christian? It makes no difference what your answer is. When you really think about spending all eternity in heaven, "our present sufferings are not worth comparing with the glory that will be revealed in us" (Romans 8:18). In fact, when compared with an eternity in the perfect world of heaven, our "troubles" are actually "light and momentary" (2 Corinthians 4:17). There is no comparison between 90 years here and never-ending glory in heaven!

Thinking that way gives us a better perspective. The devil and this world afflict and attack us and seek to destroy our faith. Our own sinful flesh betrays us and seeks to lead us astray. Nevertheless, we want to "be faithful" to our Savior, "even to the point of death" because we know that he will give us "the crown of life" (Revelation 2:10).

No more tears

Years ago, a certain commercial claimed that buying a certain shampoo meant "no more tears." While that shampoo might have been a little less irritating to the eyes, it could not take away the tears that flow from the sorrows and sadness in this sin-wrecked world. But God promises to wipe away our tears when we get to heaven. Isaiah 25:8 proclaims this boldly: "He will swallow up death forever. The Sovereign LORD will wipe away the tears from all faces; he will remove the disgrace of his people from all the earth. The LORD has spoken."

This same thought is repeated in Revelation 7:17: "God will wipe away every tear from their eyes." And we read it yet one more time near the end of the Bible: "He will wipe every tear from their eyes. There will be no more death or mourning or crying or pain, for the old order of things has passed away" (21:4). Since death, sadness, and all of the effects of sin will be left behind, we will have no reason to shed tears in heaven.

The fact that God mentions he will wipe away every tear has something to say about our earthly life. We will shed tears here. We Christians are not exempt from the common sorrows and setbacks in this life. We too experience sadness at the death of a loved one. It is not a sin to shed tears, for our Lord was perfect and yet we read that "Jesus wept" (John 11:35). It's great to know that we will shed no tears of sadness in heaven!

No more hunger or thirst

I am like many Americans. I do not know what it's like to be truly hungry. There has not been a single day in my entire life when my family has not had food. Some people have faced more difficult days than I have. Some have struggled to find enough food to eat. Some who live in the desert know what it is like to be really in need of water. They know what it's like to have the sun beat on them.

People who have faced such difficulties can appreciate the promise that when believers arrive safely in heaven, "They will neither hunger nor thirst, nor will the desert heat or the sun beat upon them" (Isaiah 49:10). Since most of my life has been spent in a northern climate, I did not really comprehend these words until I spent a year in Phoenix, Arizona. When the temperature reached 123 degrees Fahrenheit, I better understood what it means to have the sun really beat upon you. The climate in parts of Palestine is similar to that of Arizona. God's people could appreciate this promise. They would have relief in heaven. Revelation 7:16 says, "Never again will they hunger; never again will they thirst. The sun will not beat upon them, nor any scorching heat."

Sometimes people ask what the temperature will be in heaven. We are not told, but we know that we will not be too hot or too cold. We will be in perfect comfort for all eternity.

No more of sin's consequences

When we get to heaven, we will never have to suffer any of sin's consequences ever again. Heaven's residents don't have to suffer any of the troubles brought by sin because, for them, *the old order of things* has passed away" (Revelation 21:4). Just think of all the consequences of sin that we will not have to experience ever again, once we reach our home in heaven. God will provide eternal relief from all the difficulties we face because sin entered this world. When we get to heaven, there will be no more wars. There will be no more fighting of any kind. It will be good not to have to endure family squabbles or petty quarrels. We will not be sinners. We will not have to deal with sinners. We will not have difficult days at work. We will not be anxious or nervous. We will not become depressed. We will not experience loss. We will not have to take medicine. We will not need to go to a doctor at all. We will be perfectly healthy. We will not suffer the effects of sinful aging. We will never attend another funeral because there will be no death there! As we read from Scripture, we will not need to worry about food and drink either.

Some say that we will not eat or drink in heaven. I think that is probably saying more than the Bible does. We will not lack food and drink. It is possible that we will enjoy food and drink. (See chapter 8 on "Wedding banquet/feast" and study Matthew 26:29; Luke 22:30; and Matthew 8:11). This is how Luther described heaven to his son John in a letter:

> I know of a pretty, beautiful, [and] cheerful garden where there are many children wearing little golden coats. [They] pick up fine apples, pears, cherries, [and] yellow and blue plums under the trees; they sing, jump, and are merry. They also have nice ponies with golden reins and silver saddles.[45]

Luther obviously tried to make heaven seem most appealing to his son. We know that we will be eternally joyful in heaven. Eating and drinking could be a part of that enjoyment. But the best part about heaven is that we will be with God.

With the Lord forever

We know that, in heaven, "We will be *with the Lord* forever" (1 Thessalonians 4:17). This will be the greatest blessing for us in heaven, to be with our Savior and see his face forever. God's Word points to this again and again.

Jesus prepared a place for us in heaven when he died on the cross and paid for all our sins. He said, "If I go and prepare a place for you, I will come back and take you to *be with me* that you also may be where I am" (John 14:3). The whole point of our Savior's suffering and death was that he would take us to be *with him* in heaven. Jesus said so. In his High Priestly Prayer, our Redeemer prayed, "Father, I want those you have given me to be *with me* where I am, and to see my glory, the glory you have given me because you loved me before the creation of the world" (John 17:24).

Going to heaven to be with Jesus is far better than living in this life. Jesus is with us here, but it isn't the same. Here he is invisible to us. We can't see him. In heaven, we will see him. (See chapter 8 on "Seeing God.") John wrote about this in the last chapter of the Bible:

> No longer will there be any curse. The throne of God and of the Lamb will be in the city, and his servants will serve him. *They will see his face*, and his name will be on their foreheads. There will be no more night. They will not need the light of a lamp or the light of the sun, for the Lord God will give them light. And they will reign for ever and ever. (Revelation 22:3-5)

The curse of sin will be long gone. The Lamb of God, Jesus, who took away the sins of the world, will be there. All believers and angels will serve God. Believers will see his face. Yes, we will see God's face in heaven. We will belong to him. We won't need the sun, moon, or stars anymore because God himself will provide the light. He will shine with glory. And we believers will reign there. We will rule for ever and ever!

Since the curse of sin will be gone in heaven, we will be free from all of the terrible consequences of sin. Knowing and believing these words, we join Paul in saying that we "would prefer to be away from the body and at home with the Lord" (2 Corinthians 5:8). Yes, by faith in Jesus our Savior, we "desire to depart and be with Christ, which is better by far" (Philippians 1:23).

The apostle John looked forward to being in heaven. He heard a voice from the throne say, "Now the dwelling of God is with men, and he will live with them. They will be his people, and God himself will be *with them* and be their God" (Revelation 21:3). God will be with us and live with us in heaven. In another place, John wrote, "We know that when he appears, we shall be like him, for we shall see him as he is" (1 John 3:2). The Old Testament believer Job looked forward to the time when in his flesh he would see God. He knew what would happen after he rose from death. He wrote, "I myself will see him with my own eyes—I, and not another. How my heart yearns within me!" (Job 19:27). May our hearts also yearn for that time when we will be able to see God our Savior and be with him.

With our fellow believers

We will not be alone in heaven. We have heard that we will be with God. Our fellow believers will be there too. The Bible mentions this fact in quite a few passages. Jesus said that "many will come from the east and the west, and will take their places at the feast *with Abraham, Isaac and Jacob* in the kingdom of heaven" (Matthew 8:11). There will be many believers in heaven. They will come from *the east* and *the west,* from all points on the globe. They will join Abraham, Isaac, and Jacob. Old Testament believers will be with New Testament believers at the great feast in heaven.

Jesus spoke of this as a warning to unbelievers, but we can learn much from these words too: "There will be weeping there, and gnashing of teeth, when you see Abraham, Isaac and Jacob and all the prophets in the kingdom of God, but you yourselves thrown out. People will come from east and west and north and south, and will take their places at the feast in the kingdom of God" (Luke 13:28,29).

Unbelievers will weep and gnash their teeth at this sight. The Old Testament patriarchs will be in heaven. All the prophets will be there too! These were the very prophets who were despised and abused. These faithful preachers of God's pure Word will be in heaven forever. This is encouraging for God's servants today! Although the unbelievers will be thrown out, the faithful prophets will be in God's kingdom forever.

Don't give up, faithful preachers and teachers! Don't give up, faithful Christians! Believers will enter heaven from east and west and north and south. The gospel will be preached in the whole world before the end of the world. By God's power in his Word, faith will come from "hearing the message" of the gospel (Romans 10:17), and there will be believers from all over the world. These believers from all different nationalities, languages, and cultural backgrounds will enter the same heaven as Abraham, Isaac, Jacob, and all the prophets. When Jesus shed his blood and died on the cross, he "purchased men for God from every tribe and language and people and nation" (Revelation 5:9).

The church triumphant, the heavenly Jerusalem

We call the entire group of all believers in Jesus the holy Christian church, the invisible church, or simply,

the church. Believers who are still living in this sinful
world, contending for the faith, are part of the church
militant. These believers are still fighting the good fight
of faith. Believers who have entered heaven are part of
the church triumphant. Scripture has still other names
for the church. Galatians 4:26 refers to the church as "the
Jerusalem that is above." Hebrews 12:22 says, "You have
come to Mount Zion, to the heavenly Jerusalem, the city
of the living God. You have come to thousands upon
thousands of angels in joyful assembly." These words
describe the congregation of all believers, the number of
which is known only to God. These words are not talking
about the earthly Mount Zion on which the earthly city
of Jerusalem was built. They are talking about the heavenly Jerusalem, the city of the living God. God dwells
among his people. This is already true now, but we cannot see it. We believers are already in joyful fellowship
with our fellow believers, but in heaven we will realize
this more completely. We will see and know our fellow
believers. The invisible church will become visible to all
of us. When Jesus returns, we will finally know for sure
who is with us and who isn't. John was afforded a vision
of this. In Revelation 21:2, he wrote, "I saw the Holy
City, the new Jerusalem, coming down out of heaven
from God, prepared as a bride beautifully dressed for her
husband." These words are part of a vision. In figurative
language, Scripture tells us what we have already learned.
On the Last Day, when Jesus returns, "God will bring
with Jesus those who have fallen asleep in him" (1 Thessalonians 4:14). We will see our fellow believers. These
terms "the Holy City" and "the new Jerusalem" describe
the church triumphant, so we sometimes use these as
terms for heaven itself. Yet the heavenly Jerusalem does

not so much describe a place as it does the congregation of all true believers.

Great multitude

We really don't know how many believers are alive today, let alone how many have lived in the past. But when we finally see all of these believers with Jesus, it will be a very impressive sight indeed! In another vision, earlier in the book of Revelation, John saw the great multitude of believers in heaven. He wrote, "After this I looked and there before me was a *great multitude* that no one could count, from every nation, tribe, people and language, standing before the throne and in front of the Lamb. They were wearing white robes and were holding palm branches in their hands" (Revelation 7:9). These believers praised our Savior in a loud voice. These believers are in heaven because "they have washed their robes and made them white in the blood of the Lamb" (verse 14). Jesus won forgiveness for them. They have good reason to serve and worship God day and night for all eternity in heaven.

The Jehovah's Witnesses teach that only 144,000 people will go to heaven to reign with Jesus. They see this as a literal number, but the book of Revelation is filled with pictures and symbolic language. The book of Revelation itself reveals that this is not a literal number when it says that the number of the people in heaven is "a great multitude that no one could count."

Will we recognize one another?

When we get to heaven, we will live with our fellow believers forever! It is difficult to imagine exactly what this will be like. Will we recognize one another? I am convinced that we will. We will certainly keep our same identities in heaven, even after we are glorified. In the account of our Savior's transfiguration, the disciples recognized Moses and Elijah. Peter even mentioned their names when he said to Jesus, "Lord, it is good for us to be here. If you wish, I will put up three shelters—one for you, one for Moses and one for Elijah" (Matthew 17:4). It is good for us to be here! That's what we will say when we finally reach our heavenly home. It's great to be here! It will be great to be with our fellow believers in heaven. But we won't be the only ones in heaven.

With the holy angels

In heaven, we will join the company of the heavenly host. We will be with the holy angels. Hebrews 12:22 says that the heavenly Jerusalem has "thousands upon thousands of angels in joyful assembly." While we are on earth, we have already joined this group spiritually by faith. In heaven, we will see them and be among them visibly. In heaven, we will join the angels in worshiping God our Savior in holy bliss and perfection (Revelation 5:11; 7:11).

Like the holy angels

We will join the angels in worship, but we will not become angels. Scripture reveals that we will be like angels, because we will not be married in heaven. Jesus says, "At the resurrection people will neither marry nor be given in marriage; they will be like the angels in heaven" (Matthew 22:30). We will be like the angels in that we will not be married or get married.

We will be like the angels in another respect; we will not die. Jesus says, "Those who are considered worthy of taking part in that age and in the resurrection from the dead will neither marry nor be given in marriage, and they can no longer die; for they are like the angels" (Luke 20:35,36).

Sometimes well-intended Christians are misled by television programs and movies. They begin to think that when we die, we will become angels. So we need to repeat for clarity: We will not become angels! We will be like angels in the following two ways: (1) we will not be married, and (2) we will not die.

The image of God—restored

Though the holy image of God was lost in the fall into sin, we will once again live perfectly in the image of God in heaven. The image of God is being renewed now in the new nature of believers (Ephesians 4:24; Colossians 3:10). But, when we get to heaven, the old sinful nature (old Adam) will be gone forever. We will have perfect knowledge of God's will, and we will be able to follow it perfectly. The inspired apostle John wrote, "We know that when he appears, we shall be like him, for we shall see him as he is" (1 John 3:2). We will be like God when we see him—perfect and without any sin. We will live in the new self forever.

Full knowledge

As we've been studying heaven, we have occasionally mentioned how little we really know about heaven. Once we get there, we will know what it is like from experience. We will know much more there than we do here. In 1 Corinthians 13:12, the inspired apostle wrote, "Now we see but a poor reflection as in a mirror; then we shall see face to face. Now I know in part; then I shall know fully, even as I am fully known." In heaven we will understand completely what now we only know in part.

We won't need to study the Bible in heaven. But we do need to know what the Bible says here. We do not graduate from studying the Bible until God calls us home to heaven. When we are there, we will not need the Bible to tell us about God. We will know. The image of God will be perfectly restored. Like Adam and Eve in the Garden of Eden, we will have perfect knowledge of God's will and the ability to do God's will without sin. Only we will never fall into sin again.

Holiness

Jesus washed away our sins so that when we arrive in heaven, we believers will be "a radiant church, without stain or wrinkle or any other blemish, but holy and blameless" (Ephesians 5:27). None of our past sins will be remembered. Romans 8:1 says, "There is now no condemnation for those who are in Christ Jesus." When we rise from death, we will be perfect, holy, and righteous. Psalm 17:15 says, "And I—in righteousness I will see your face; when I awake, I will be satisfied with seeing your likeness." We will stand before God in righteousness. We will be completely satisfied in seeing God. We will want this to last forever.

"No one will take away your joy"

The good news is that heaven does last forever! As we have learned, "we will be with the Lord forever" (1 Thessalonians 4:17). With the Lord, we will have every good thing. Jesus said to his disciples, "Now is your time of grief, but I will see you again and you will rejoice, and *no one will take away your joy*" (John 16:22). Once we arrive in heaven, no one will take away our joy.

We keep returning to that well-known passage John 3:16, because it gives us such clear answers. Notice how long we will be in heaven. "God so loved the world that he gave his one and only Son, that whoever believes in him shall not perish but have *eternal* life." We will live for all eternity in heaven (Matthew 25:46). We will be with our Savior and enjoy the perfect world of heaven forever. When we believers die, we do go to a happier place.

Degrees of glory

Every believer will enjoy heaven. There will not be degrees of joy (bliss) in heaven. But will there be degrees of glory in heaven? Some have found the answer in Daniel 12:3, "Those who are wise will shine like the brightness of the heavens, and those who lead many to righteousness, like the stars for ever and ever." Will some believers shine more brightly with glory in heaven? Might it be that those who lead many to righteousness will have special glory there?

In the parable of the ten minas, the king rewards his faithful servants with different amounts. The servant who earned ten more minas was given ten cities, while the servant who earned five more minas was given five cities (Luke 19:17,19). Might this indicate that our King will hand out different degrees of glory in heaven?

First Corinthians 15:40-42 describes the difference in glory between earthly and heavenly bodies:

> There are also heavenly bodies and there are earthly bodies; but the splendor of the heavenly bodies is one kind, and the splendor of the earthly bodies is another. The sun has one kind of splendor, the moon another and the stars another; and star differs from star in splendor.
>
> So will it be with the resurrection of the dead. The body that is sown is perishable, it is raised imperishable.

Commenting on these verses, Luther wrote:

> Many differences or degrees of glory will prevail among us.
> For instance, Peter's and Paul's will be the glory of apos-
> tles; one person will partake of the glory of a martyr,
> another of that of a pious bishop or preacher; each one in
> accord with the works which he has performed. Similarly,
> each member of the body has its own honor, the eyes have
> an honor that differs from that of the hands or feet, etc.;
> moreover, the sun in the heavens has a brilliance different
> from that of the stars, and one star is brighter and more
> radiant than another, making each nicely distinct from
> the other. And yet with regard to person they are alike
> and they have the same essence, and all will have equal
> joy and bliss in God.[46]

Luther mentions that this difference in glory will be in
accord with the works we have performed. He is, of
course, talking there about fruits of faith. Scripture also
mentions fruits of faith in these terms in Revelation 14:13:
"Blessed are the dead who die in the Lord from now on.
Yes, . . . they will rest from their labor, for their deeds will
follow them." "Their deeds" refers to the fruits of faith the
Holy Spirit produces through believers. "Their labor" may
refer to their serving the Lord by proclaiming God's Word,
as in other places of Scripture. (See John 4:38; 1 Corinthians 3:8 and 15:58; Philippians 2:16; Colossians 1:29; and
1 Timothy 5:17.)

Luther insisted that people are saved by faith in Christ,
without their works. And yet, on the basis of Scripture,
Luther did not regard fruits of faith as useless:

> There will be distinctions made also in yonder life,
> depending upon how a person worked and lived here. For
> instance, since St. Paul was an apostle and Samuel and
> Isaiah prophets, and so forth, these will enjoy greater glory

than others as men who did more and suffered more in their offices. Similarly, pious Sarah or Rachel will be preeminent before other women and yet will not be a different being or life. Thus everybody will be distinguished and honored in accordance with his office, and yet there will be one God and Lord in all, and there will be identical happiness and bliss. With regard to person, no one will be more or have more than another, St. Peter no more than you or I. Yet there must be a distinction on the basis of works. For God did not effect through St. Paul what he effected through Isaiah, and vice versa. Therefore all will bring their works with them by which they will shine and praise God; and it will be said that St. Peter wrought more than I or others did. This man or this woman lived in this way and accomplished so much. In short, before God all will be alike in faith and grace and heavenly essence; but there will be a difference in works and their glory.[47]

When I think of the people I would like to meet in heaven, I think of some of the very people Luther mentions. Yet, let's try to separate what we know for certain from Scripture and what is less clear.

Here's what we know for sure. We know that all glory really belongs to God. He deserves all of our praise. In heaven, our praise will be directed to him. There will be heroes of faith in heaven. Some of them are mentioned in Hebrews chapter 11. Yet, if these heroes of faith shine brighter or have more outward glory than you and I have, we can be sure that they will not have more joy there than you and I will. (See Matthew 20:1-16.) We can be sure that there will be no envy or jealousy there, because there will be no sin in heaven.

Some Christian theologians seem to teach very confidently about this matter of different degrees of glory, but the truth is that there is much that we do not know for

sure. Scripture is very clear about degrees of punishment
in hell, but is it as clear about degrees of glory in heaven?
Dr. Becker wrote, "The teaching of Scripture is not as
clear on the situation in heaven in this regard as it is on
that in hell."[48] When Revelation 20:4 mentions "thrones
on which were seated those who had been given authority
to judge" that could refer to differences in authority. And
when the same verse mentions that John saw "the souls of
those who had been beheaded because of their testimony
for Jesus and because of the word of God" it might very
well be revealing that martyrs will have special glory in
heaven. That seems to be the case, but what will the differences really be and how are we to understand this?

When we see God's creation, we see great variety, and
each type of plant, animal, bird, and fish has its own type of
"glory." Should we think of it that way? We see a beautiful
eagle flying and give glory to God. We see a stately tree and
praise God who made it. Each has its own type of glory. Is
that how it will be in heaven? It seems likely that we will
marvel at the faith God gave to Abraham, the mission
work God enabled Paul to do, and the glorious faithfulness
God worked in the martyrs. (See Revelation 14:13.)

Only God knows for sure who is a hero of faith. Jesus
said, "I tell you the truth: Among those born of women
there has not risen anyone greater than John the Baptist;
yet he who is least in the kingdom of heaven is greater
than he" (Matthew 11:11). Read our Savior's words
recorded in (Matthew 20:1-16), concluding with his statement in verse 16: "So the last will be first, and the first
will be last." How does that affect our understanding of
degrees of glory?

Reading that section of Scripture along with the one
that comes before it (the end of Matthew chapter 19)

reminds me that Jesus was not in the habit of simply satis-
fying people's curious questions about heaven. He was certainly in the habit of offering correction or comfort as he
saw the need. When his disciples needed encouragement,
he informed them of their glorious future reward in
heaven. When they might have wondered if they would
have more joy than others, he corrected their view
through the parable of the workers in the vineyard. Even
those who are brought to faith just before they die will
experience the full joy of heaven. They will receive the
same eternal life as those who "have borne the burden of
the work and the heat of the day" (Matthew 20:12).
When his disciples expect extra, Jesus reminds them of
equal joy. When his servants are weary and discouraged,
he reminds them of unbelievable rewards at the renewal of
all things. Though we don't deserve it, God gives us an
eternal reward in heaven.

From time to time, people have asked me why I became
a pastor. With no harm intended, they seem to suggest
that I might have accomplished a little more in another
occupation. Some think that maybe I could have made
more money if I would have been a lawyer. Maybe I could
have lived near my parents and relatives if I would have
become something else. Sometimes some people, and
even called workers in moments of weakness, look at the
visible rewards for serving full time in the public ministry
and wonder if it's worth it. I don't need to explain to
called workers what I'm talking about here. Then, when I
think of all the birthday parties I've missed, how I didn't
get to spend Thanksgiving or Christmas with my parents
and other relatives, simply because I'm a pastor and was
called by God to serve far from home, I think of what
Jesus says in this next Bible passage. Peter had just

watched a rich young man walk away from Jesus because he loved his possessions too much. Jesus had just mentioned what a great miracle it is when someone believes. It is impossible for man but possible for God to bring someone to faith. Then we read the following words:

> Peter answered him, "We have left everything to follow you! What then will there be for us?"
>
> Jesus said to them, "I tell you the truth, at the renewal of all things, when the Son of Man sits on his glorious throne, you who have followed me will also sit on twelve thrones, judging the twelve tribes of Israel. And everyone who has left houses or brothers or sisters or father or mother or children or fields for my sake will receive a hundred times as much and will inherit eternal life. But many who are first will be last, and many who are last will be first." (Matthew 19:27-30)

There is more in there than meets the eye in a superficial reading. Those who have been called to serve far from their own mothers, fathers, brothers, and sisters will receive a hundred times as much in heaven. I don't know exactly what that means, but I know that it is true. If you have been called to serve your Savior far from your home, far from your father and mother, you can be sure that, by faith in Christ, you will receive a hundred times as much and will inherit eternal life.

Jesus said that many who are first will be last, and many who are last will be first. This reminds me of the widow's mite. So many seem to be doing so much, and giving so much, that we begin to think that they are doing the most or giving the most. But we don't know that. The Lord knows the truth, and the truth might not be what it seems. Consider this real-life example:

Jesus sat down opposite the place where the offerings were put and watched the crowd putting their money into the temple treasury. Many rich people threw in large amounts. But a poor widow came and put in two very small copper coins, worth only a fraction of a penny.

Calling his disciples to him, Jesus said, "I tell you the truth, this poor widow has put more into the treasury than all the others. They all gave out of their wealth; but she, out of her poverty, put in everything—all she had to live on." (Mark 12:41-44)

The widow gave more than all the others, though the amount was very small by comparison. By faith, she gave the Lord one hundred percent. No outsider would have noticed. Jesus did.

When we think of those who seem to be serving the most, we might think of called workers. But we must not forget the humble, silent service of many dedicated Christians who may receive little attention. They might work to keep the church looking nice or reach out to their neighbors. With their prayers and offerings, they generously support the preaching and teaching of God's Word at home and all around the world. We should not worry about who will be first or last in heaven. Let us only be sure that we are faithful to our Savior.

It will be great to be there. While we are here, may we make the most of our time, talents, and treasures to serve the Lord. In the end, may we be found faithful to our faithful Savior.

Around the throne, a glorious band,
The saints in countless numbers stand,
Of ev'ry tongue, redeemed to God,
Arrayed in garments washed in blood.

Through tribulation great they came;
They bore the cross, despised the shame.
From all their labors now they rest
In God's eternal glory blest. (CW 549:1,2)

11

We Can Be Sure of Eternal Life!

When we say, "I hope that it doesn't rain tomorrow," we are not sure if it will rain or not. We are only stating what we wish might happen. Genuine Christian hope is not a mere wish.

When Christians say, "I hope I go to heaven," what do they mean? If they mean this in the sense that they are not sure if they will go to heaven or not but that they hope that they might enter heaven, this reveals weak faith. This type of "hope" is not the Christian hope taught in the Bible. Christian hope reveals a strong faith and a certain confidence that God will keep his promise.

Christian hope

Let us examine some Bible passages to learn what is meant by the term *hope* in each of them. This will lead us to a clearer understanding of what Christian hope is. Romans 8:24,25 reveals that *hope* means waiting for something patiently. "For in this hope we were saved. But hope that is seen is no hope at all. Who hopes for what he already has? But if we *hope* for what we do not *yet* have, we wait for it patiently." We hope for what we do not yet have. We wait patiently for God to keep his promises. But, by faith, we are sure that he will keep his promises. Second Corinthians 3:12 explains that "since we have such a hope, we are very bold." We are not uncertain. We are bold and confident, knowing that God will keep his promises. We believers have "a faith and knowledge resting on the hope of eternal life, which God, who does not lie, promised before the beginning of time" (Titus 1:2). Our Christian hope is based on God, who does not lie. It is based on the promises God has given to us in the Scriptures.

In that sense, hope becomes *faith directed toward the future*. Just as faith is sure of God's Word and believes it, so hope is sure of God's Word about the future and believes that what God has promised will happen. Since God has promised eternal life to all who believe in Jesus, we have "the *hope* of eternal life" (Titus 3:7). When our believing loved ones die, we might be sad, but we do not need to "grieve like the rest of men, who have no hope" (1 Thessalonians 4:13). We have hope. We know that God keeps his promises. We know that God took the soul of our believing loved one to heaven. We know that God will raise this person's body on the Last Day.

Christian hope is closely connected to faith in 1 Peter 1:21, which says, "Your *faith* and *hope* are in God." First Peter 1:13 makes hope sound just like faith when it says,

"Set your *hope* fully on the grace to be given you when Jesus Christ is revealed." By faith, we look forward to our Savior's return and our heavenly summons. That is our Christian hope. It is sure and certain. It is *faith directed toward the future, based on God's promises.*

First Timothy 6:17 seems to use the term *hope* in a place where we might expect the term *faith.* It says, "Command those who are rich in this present world not to be arrogant nor to put their *hope* in wealth, which is so uncertain, but to put their *hope* in God, who richly provides us with everything for our enjoyment." We might expect it to say put their *faith* in God, but it says, "put their *hope* in God." Christian hope is sure and certain trust in God's promises for the future.

Christian hope is not uncertain wishing, as in "I hope my team wins the World Series."

Notice how the term *hope* is used in Hebrews 6:18,19: "God did this so that, by two unchangeable things in which it is impossible for God to lie, we who have fled to take hold of the hope offered to us may be greatly encouraged. We have this *hope* as an *anchor* for the soul, *firm and secure.*" We might expect the term "promise of God" to be used in place of *hope.* God's promises are an "anchor for the soul." God's promises are "firm and secure." Since our hope rests on God's promises, it is as firm and secure as God's promises.

"Let us hold fast the confession of our *hope* without wavering, for He who promised is faithful" (Hebrews 10:23, NKJV). Our hope is based on our God's Word, which we confess. We might expect it to say confession of our *faith,* but it says, "confession of our *hope.*" Let us hold on to this *hope,* this *faith directed to the future,* without wavering. And the reason why we can be sure and certain is that he who promised is faithful. God always keeps his promises.

According to 1 Peter 1:3, this hope is a living hope. "Praise be to the God and Father of our Lord Jesus Christ! In his great mercy he has given us new birth into a *living hope* through the resurrection of Jesus Christ from the dead." God has caused us to be born again into a living hope. We have the hope of eternal life, the sure and certain confidence that because Jesus lives, we too shall live.

So Scripture urges us to reach out to others. "Always be prepared to give an answer to everyone who asks you to give the reason for the *hope* that you have" (1 Peter 3:15). Always be ready to tell others about what gives you confidence as you look toward the future. You know the answer, don't you? You know that you are going to heaven by faith in Jesus! Tell them the way to heaven. Tell them what they need to know so that they too can look ahead with confidence to the return of our Savior.

Are you sure that you are going to heaven? Some might say, "I hope so," and yet not be sure. You know that Christian hope is certain; it is faith directed to the future, based on God's promise.

> My *hope* is built on nothing less
> Than Jesus' blood and righteousness;
> I dare to make no other claim
> But wholly lean on Jesus' name.
> On Christ, the solid rock, I stand;
> All other ground is sinking sand. (CW 382:1)

Be sure that you are going to heaven!

We do not have to be doubtful about whether or not God will receive us into his heavenly kingdom. Yes, we are sinners. Yes, we deserve to perish based on our own sinful thoughts, words, and actions.

But God saved us. "For God so loved the world that he gave his one and only Son, that whoever believes in him shall not perish but have eternal life" (John 3:16). Just think about that! God loved the whole world so much that he sent Jesus to live a perfect life in the place of every sinner and to die on the cross as the substitute for every sinner.

God placed all of our sins on Jesus. "We all, like sheep, have gone astray [into sin], each of us has turned to his own [sinful] way; and the LORD has laid on him the iniquity [the sins] of us all" (Isaiah 53:6). On Calvary's cross, Jesus received the full weight and guilt of the sins of the world. There he paid our price in full. There Jesus made atonement for our sins. First John 2:2 informs us that "he is the atoning sacrifice for our sins, and not only for ours but also for the sins of the whole world." Remember, Jesus was not on that cross paying for *some* sins. He was paying for *all* sins. He rose from death because he satisfied God's justice and accomplished his mission. Jesus himself said that whoever believes in him will go to heaven. This promise gives us assurance as we look toward the future. We can be certain that our Lord will keep his promise and take us and all believers to heaven.

Since the Bible very clearly declares that Jesus did this for the whole world, we can be absolutely sure that he did it for us (even me!). If God had written each of our names in the Bible, it would be less certain. If my name was printed in Scripture, I could not be certain that God meant me and not just someone else who has the same name. But I do not need to worry about that. I know that Jesus "died for all" (2 Corinthians 5:15).

Just as all are sinners, so all are justified. "*All have sinned* and fall short of the glory of God, *and are justified* freely by his grace through the redemption that came by Christ Jesus" (Romans 3:23,24). All have sinned and are justified. The subject of "are justified" is the subject of "have sinned," that is, "All." Thus it means that all sinners are declared not guilty through Jesus. God has done this freely, without any cost to us, by his grace. The price was paid by Christ Jesus on the cross of Calvary. Whoever believes in him receives the benefits he won, namely, eternal life.

Eternal life is not something that we somehow earn. It is completely and totally a gift. "The wages of sin is death, but the gift of God is eternal life in Christ Jesus our Lord" (Romans 6:23). We can be sure that we have eternal life, thanks to Jesus our Savior.

The apostle Paul was sure that he was going to heaven. He wrote, "I know whom I have believed, and am convinced that he is able to guard what I have entrusted to him for that day" (2 Timothy 1:12). Paul was convinced that God would take care of the details so that he could arrive safely in heaven.

The reason why we can be so sure is revealed in Ephesians 5:25-27, "Christ loved the church and gave himself up for her to make her holy, cleansing her by the washing with water through the word, and to present her to himself as a radiant church, without stain or wrinkle or any other blemish, but holy and blameless." Our Lord died for us to make us holy. He washed our sins away in Holy Baptism. He is able to present us, and all believers, before his throne without any stain of sin. We can be sure that we are going to heaven because Jesus did all the work of saving us. By faith in him, we will enter heaven.

What if I am sinning when I die?

From time to time, sincere believers might wonder about the circumstances of death. They know that the old Adam constantly afflicts us. They know how prone we all are to fall into sin. They wonder if they will still go to heaven if they die while committing a sin.

First of all, this question reveals a misunderstanding of sin and how often we sin. We sin more often than we realize. Even when we think we aren't sinning, we are falling short of perfection. Who can say that they are perfect in every way during a worship service in church? We might daydream, even briefly, during the sermon. Maybe we are inattentive during the Scripture lessons. Maybe we struggle to be completely cheerful as we place our offerings in the plate. And this is while we are participating in a worship service! The truth is that we are sinning all the time! Isaiah 64:6 reveals how prevalent sin really is. "All of us have become like one who is unclean, and all our righteous acts are like filthy rags." We are all sinful. Even our best attempts are stained by sinfulness. We are falling into sin much more than we realize! We fall short of perfection all the time.

Yet we believers stand in a *state of grace* with God, thanks to Jesus. Romans 5:1,2 boldly states, "Since we have been justified through faith, we have peace with God through our Lord Jesus Christ, through whom we have gained access by faith into *this grace in which we now stand.* And we rejoice in the hope of the glory of God." The words in italic print tell us that we stand in a state of grace. We walk through life surrounded by an invisible force field of God's grace. We believers do not step in and out of this invisible sphere. We stand securely inside it. Scripture calls it "this grace in which we now stand." We call it a state of grace with God. God's grace covers us with forgiveness continually. So, we can rejoice in the hope of the glory of God. We believers can be happy, knowing that God will take us to heaven.

No matter how many times we fall short, God forgives us in Christ. No matter how many times we will fall short, God will forgive us in Christ. Romans 5:20 says, "Where sin increased, grace increased all the more." Our certainty that we are going to heaven does not rest in our weak and feeble hands but in the amazing grace of God.

We should never sin on purpose. We should never regard sin lightly. This would be incompatible with the faith that lives in our hearts. But we should not be afraid that we might be sinning when we die. We live in a state of grace. We are forgiven through Christ. We believers can be sure that heaven is ours.

Is it still possible for me to fall away and perish?

You may have noticed that I said, "We believers can be sure." This prompts another question that troubles some sincere Christians. They wonder if it is possible for believers to fall away from faith. The simplest answer is "Yes, it is possible that a believer could fall from faith." The Bible does not teach a "once a believer, always a believer" doctrine. That came through false teachers.

The Bible answers this question from two different perspectives. Knowing which perspective to apply in a given case requires the ability to properly distinguish between the law and the gospel of God.

The perspective of the *law:* God warns us not to stray from our Savior and his Word, because it is possible that we could fall from saving faith.

The perspective of the *gospel:* God comforts us with the assurance that he will guard and keep us and be faithful to his promises.

First Corinthians 10:12 provides the perspective of God's law: "If you think you are standing firm, be careful that you don't fall!" Here God's Word warns us against arrogance and carnal security. We should not trust ourselves or rely on our own ability to stay with God.

Jude 24,25 provides the perspective of God's gospel: "To him *who is able to keep you from falling* and to present you before his glorious presence without fault and with great joy—to the only God our Savior be glory, majesty, power and authority, through Jesus Christ our Lord, before all ages, now and forevermore! Amen." Here God's Word comforts us believers with the good news that God can keep us from falling. Trust God and his ability to keep us with him.

God is able to keep us from falling. The following illustration makes those words particularly vivid in my mind. Perhaps you will agree.

> On a cold winter day, when the sidewalks were covered with ice, a pastor and his little boy were on their way to church. It was the first time three-year-old Bobby was wearing an overcoat in which there were deep pockets. As they approached a slippery place, the father extended his hand to the youngster and said: "You'd better let me hold your hand." But the boy's hands were snug in his pockets, and he kept them there—until he slipped and fell! Somewhat humbled by this experience, he raised himself and said: "I'll hold your hand, Daddy." And he reached up and took his father's hand with the feeble grasp of a three-year-old.
>
> Soon they came to another slippery place—and down he went! His tiny fingers had not been able to grip his

father's hand with sufficient strength to insure against his
fall. Once more he picked himself up and they resumed
their walk. But after a moment's reflection Bobby looked
up into his father's face and said with a childlike confidence: "YOU hold MY hand, Daddy." And as they went
safely on their way and ultimately reached their destina-
tion, it was the father's hand that upheld the lad and pre-
served him from further danger. Not the boy's grip on the
father's hand, but the father's grip on his!

Similarly, your continuing in the faith is not so much a matter of your holding on to God as it is a matter of God holding on to you. And you have His promise that He will.[49]

May these words give you some comfort if you are
afraid that you might fall from faith. God is able to keep
you from falling, as you continue to feed your faith by
regularly receiving the gospel in Word and sacrament.
Don't be afraid, dear believer. God is able to keep you
from falling.

So, the Bible answers the question from the perspective
of the law and the perspective of the gospel. From the perspective of the law, the Bible says, "If you live according to
the sinful nature, you will die" (Romans 8:13). From the
perspective of the gospel, the Bible says, "There is now no
condemnation for those who are in Christ Jesus" (8:1).
God's Word reassures us:

In the same way, the Spirit helps us in our weakness. We
do not know what we ought to pray for, but the Spirit
himself intercedes for us with groans that words cannot
express. And he who searches our hearts knows the mind
of the Spirit, because the Spirit intercedes for the saints in
accordance with God's will.

And we know that in all things God works for the good of
those who love him, who have been called according to

his purpose. For those God foreknew he also predestined to be conformed to the likeness of his Son, that he might be the firstborn among many brothers. And those he predestined, he also called; those he called, he also justified; those he justified, he also glorified. (Romans 8:26-30)

Notice how, from the gospel's perspective, our salvation depends entirely on God. God has done it all. God is taking care of it. God will help you and keep you in his loving care. He has it all under control.

Who shall separate us from the love of Christ? Shall trouble or hardship or persecution or famine or nakedness or danger or sword? As it is written: "For your sake we face death all day long; we are considered as sheep to be slaughtered." No, in all these things we are more than conquerors through him who loved us. For I am convinced that neither death nor life, neither angels nor demons, neither the present nor the future, nor any powers, neither height nor depth, nor anything else in all creation, will be able to separate us from the love of God that is in Christ Jesus our Lord. (Romans 8:35-39)

Those words are so comforting! Nothing can separate us from God's love in Christ!

But, then, as we read on in our Bibles we will again see the perspective of the law. We need to hear the law too. Sometimes our old Adam gets the best of us. We might become lazy in feeding our faith. We might even skip out on worship services. This is serious! When we enter the danger zone, we need a warning. We must never think it is acceptable to sin on purpose.

Let us not give up meeting together, as some are in the habit of doing, but let us encourage one another—and all the more as you see the Day approaching.

> If we deliberately keep on sinning after we have received the knowledge of the truth, no sacrifice for sins is left, but only a fearful expectation of judgment and of raging fire that will consume the enemies of God. (Hebrews 10:25-27)

This is frightening. God has our attention. But soon we are again wrapped up in fear. We need the gospel perspective. Jesus is ready to help.

> "Do not let your hearts be troubled. Trust in God; trust also in me. In my Father's house are many rooms; if it were not so, I would have told you. I am going there to prepare a place for you. And if I go and prepare a place for you, I will come back and take you to be with me that you also may be where I am. . . . I am the way and the truth and the life. No one comes to the Father except through me." (John 14:1-3,6)

The gospel calls and enables us to trust God. Then we can look forward to our heavenly summons, as did Paul, who wrote, "The Lord will rescue me from every evil attack and will bring me safely to his heavenly kingdom" (2 Timothy 4:18). Paul trusted in God, not in himself.

Before long, we again fall into various sins and we begin to feel guilty. Our consciences accuse us. First John 3:20 explains that "if our heart condemns us, God is greater than our heart, and knows all things" (NKJV). God has declared us forgiven through Christ. We are forgiven, whether our consciences quiet down right away or not. We can tell an overactive conscience, "God has forgiven me. The matter is done." Rest assured, you are forgiven through Christ. Rest assured, dear believer, heaven is open to you, thanks to Jesus.

Confirmed in bliss

Once we get to heaven, there is no chance that we will ever fall away again. We will be confirmed in holiness and bliss forever. We will be like the holy angels, who will never fall away. Our dear Savior said in Luke 20:35,36, "Those who are considered worthy of taking part in that age and in the resurrection from the dead will neither marry nor be given in marriage, and *they can no longer die; for they are like the angels.*" In heaven, God's will is always done, as Jesus revealed in the way he taught us to pray: "Your will be done on earth as it is in heaven" (Matthew 6:10). We will always do God's will in heaven, just as the holy angels always do.

On judgment day, Jesus will take his believers to "eternal life" (Matthew 25:46). Our life with Jesus in heaven will never end. We will never fall away. Just as the angels are called "elect angels" in 1 Timothy 5:21, we too will be revealed as God's elect. Like the holy angels, we will be confirmed in bliss and be holy forever.

We will never leave heaven. Revelation 3:12 reveals this comforting truth. "Him who overcomes I will make a pillar in the temple of my God. *Never again* will he leave it." Once we arrive safely in heaven, we will never want to leave. And we never will leave. We will be confirmed in bliss and never fall away.

Because it is possible that we could fall away here before we arrive safely there, we sing:

> Grant that your Spirit's help to me be always given
> Lest I should fall again and lose the way to heaven.
> Grant that he give me strength in my infirmity;
> May he renew my heart to serve you willingly.

Lord, you have raised me up to joy and exultation
And clearly shown the way that leads me to salvation.
My sins are washed away; for this I thank you, Lord.
Now with my heart and soul all evil I abhor.

(CW 460:4,3)

12

Common Questions and Answers

This study of death, heaven, and hell certainly has not answered every question. In this chapter, let's consider some questions that people commonly ask. We'll look for scriptural help and guidance. The Bible is always to be the basis of our faith and life. If you have further questions, please ask your pastor.

What will I say to the grieving family at a funeral home?
From time to time, nearly all of us visit a funeral home. When a neighbor, relative, or friend dies, we might wonder what we will say at a funeral home or funeral service. In some cases, we can say more than in others. Here is the key to knowing what to say: *determine if there is any*

evidence that the deceased had saving faith in Jesus Christ. We cannot look into a person's heart. Only God knows if that person really was a believer or not. But sometimes there is clear evidence that gives us a strong indication of what to say. For example, we might consider a person's church membership. Was this person an active member of a Christian church? Which one? What did this person seem to believe? Did this person confess faith in Jesus as the Savior from sin? Did this person seem to rely on good works to obtain God's favor? Sometimes it will be very clear. Other times it might be very doubtful. Yet, considering what this person seemed to believe does make a big difference in knowing what to say at the funeral home.

Jesus says, "Whoever believes and is baptized will be saved, but whoever does not believe will be condemned" (Mark 16:16). So, if it seems that this person really was a believer in Jesus Christ, you could talk about the deceased going to heaven. You could say that this believer is happier now. You could provide much comfort. On the other hand, if it seems that this person was not a believer, you should not speak the same way. We do not know what is in a person's heart, but we should not give false hope if there is no reason for it. If this person died in unbelief, he or she went to hell. But only God can know for sure what is really in a person's heart.

Was the deceased an unbeliever?

Maybe he kept his lawn very neat and trimmed. Maybe she was a wonderful cook. Maybe he seemed like a pretty good guy. She might have been a wonderful neighbor. It makes no difference how much "good" a person does in outward obedience to laws without faith in Christ (civic righteousness). No amount of good works will earn eternal life for sinners. Galatians 2:16 says, "A man is not justified by observing the law, but by faith in Jesus Christ. So we, too, have put our faith in Christ Jesus that we may be justified by faith in Christ and not by observing the law, because by observing the law no one will be justified." Saying that he was a good man or she was a fine lady might only confuse matters.

We might be in doubt about what was in a person's heart, but there is no doubt about this: "Clearly no one is justified before God by the law, because, 'The righteous will live by faith'" (Galatians 3:11). No one will go to heaven by being a good man or a fine lady. Faith in Jesus is the only way to heaven.

Scripture says, "Always be prepared to give an answer to everyone who asks you to give the reason for the hope that you have. But do this with gentleness and respect" (1 Peter 3:15). We certainly will want to confess our faith as Christians, also in the funeral home. We might be able to help the survivors hear the Word so that they do not perish in unbelief. Yet we wish to speak gently and respectfully. How can we do this if the deceased did not seem to have faith in Jesus? How do we apply this principle of giving clear answers and testimony, "with gentleness and respect"?

We probably would not begin by saying, "Well, I'm sorry your loved one's in hell." That would be crass. Plus, there might be information we do not know. We do not know that person's heart. Yet, in honesty, we know that we can't go into that room and say, "Well, your loved one's in a happier place now." If we don't think the person had faith, we cannot say, "At least your friend doesn't suffer anymore." If the person died in unbelief, he or she does suffer for all eternity. But are we really sure that person died in unbelief? And is it gentle and respectful to blurt out something like that at a funeral home? These sorts of difficulties lead pastors and congregations to refuse to perform Christian funerals for just any nonmember. If we have no clear confession of faith in Jesus from that person, we cannot give the clear comfort of a Christian funeral.

In a situation like this, I try to be very cautious with my words about the person who died. I would rather try to focus my attention on the person to whom I am speaking. Is this person who is mourning the loss of a loved one a believer, still in his or her time of grace? I cannot reach the person who has died, but I might be able to reach out to one of the survivors. I want to establish a line of communication that can continue after the funeral is finished. I want to rely on God's Word to get the real work done. I would like to get to the point where I can say that Jesus Christ died on the cross to save us all from sin and that believers in him go to heaven. There are many different ways of doing this. There are many different personalities. My way might not be the same as yours, but our goals can be the same. Aim to reach out to that person who is still living. We can do nothing about the deceased, but we can certainly seek to help that person in need of comfort and direction from God's saving Word.

Was the deceased a believer?

We've looked at the really difficult situation, when we think that the person who died was probably not a believer. If the person did seem to have faith in Jesus, what could you say? This is a much easier task! We can say all of the good things that Scripture encourages us to say to comfort the survivors. We can give all glory to Jesus, who saved that person. We can mention that believers go straight to heaven. We can say that he or she doesn't suffer anymore. We can say that this person's soul went to a happier place. We can say that the departed is with Jesus now. "For God so loved the world that he gave his one and only Son, that whoever believes in him shall not perish but have eternal life" (John 3:16).

We don't need to stop there. We can even talk about the resurrection. In a similar situation, believing Martha said of her brother Lazarus, who had died in faith, "I know he will rise again in the resurrection at the last day" (John 11:24). We know that all who "believe in the Lord Jesus" are saved in God's judgment and enter heaven (Acts 16:31). We know that they go to this heavenly paradise on the day that they die (Luke 23:43). We can speak about this and comfort the survivors. We can even reach out to those who might not yet believe. We can tell them the way to heaven. By faith in Christ, they too can go where the departed went.

God wants us to speak up in this way. He doesn't want us just to be silent or to talk like worldly people do. God has given us a message of comfort in the gospel. We can praise him and give that comfort to others at the funeral home. "Praise be to the God and Father of our Lord Jesus Christ, the Father of compassion and the God of all comfort, who comforts us in all our troubles, so that we can comfort those in any trouble with the comfort we ourselves have received from God" (2 Corinthians 1:3,4). We know that, by faith in Christ, "we will be with the Lord forever," so let us "encourage each other with these words" as God urges us to do (1 Thessalonians 4:17,18). The survivors may be carrying heavy burdens. We can help! Scripture says, "Carry each other's burdens, and in this way you will fulfill the law of Christ" (Galatians 6:2).

Why are many Christian funerals conducted in church?

Scripture does not command us to have Christian funerals in church, but over the years many Christians have found it very comforting to meet in a place of worship, in the house of God, to receive comfort from God's Word. Here, we praise God our Savior, who has taken a believing loved one to heaven. Here, we listen to Bible passages that comfort and encourage the survivors. Here, we receive a message from the pastor with the same goals in mind, to praise God, to comfort and encourage the survivors, and also to reach out to any nonbelievers who might attend the service. There are various customs that some churches follow in Christian liberty, but the main reason for having a funeral in church is to return to that place where we commonly meet God and he meets us—in his Word. It may be easier to sing hymns of praise in church, where there are hymnals and an organ.

Psalm 98:1 says, "Sing to the LORD a new song, for he has done marvelous things; his right hand and his holy arm have worked salvation for him." This applies to funerals. God has done marvelous things so that this person's soul is now with Jesus. He worked salvation. Let us praise our gracious God! In a sense, a funeral service is a victory celebration. Thanks to Jesus, the departed loved one has won! It is good to sing strong hymns of praise, to sing Easter hymns, to sing hymns of comfort. Psalm 23 is helpful, but so is "I Know That My Redeemer Lives." It is not wrong to cry or be sad when a loved one has died, but we must not act as if there were no hope! We must not "grieve like the rest of men, who have no hope" (1 Thessalonians 4:13). This is what makes Christian funerals distinctive. In the midst of tears and sadness, we boldly confess our faith in God's promises! We rejoice that a believer has departed to paradise. Believers can do what Psalm 100 talks about, even at a funeral. They can "worship the LORD with gladness; come before him with joyful songs . . . give thanks to him and praise his name" (verses 2,4). There is nothing wrong with having a service in a funeral home. Some churches might be too small for some funerals. Still, when it is possible, many believers do prefer to return to the established place of worship, the house of God, for this worship service of comfort and praise.

Why don't our pastors preach eulogies?

A eulogy is a speech that praises a person, particularly a person who has died. We commonly see these on television. Someone dies and all sorts of people go to the podium and say good things about the person who died. But, notice who is being praised. The person who died is being praised.

By contrast, our pastors in their funeral sermons aim to praise God and proclaim his Word. In a sense, they eulogize Christ. This does not mean that our pastors will never mention the fruits of faith of the departed believer. Often, we do mention what the person said or did, to supply evidence that this person clearly confessed faith in Jesus (as Jesus will on the Last Day—Matthew 25:35,36). But our real aim is to glorify God and proclaim his gospel. First Corinthians 10:31 says, "Whatever you do, do it all *for the glory of God.*" Romans 11:36 says, "From him and through him and to him are all things. *To him be the glory forever!*" God and his "glorious grace" deserve all the praise when a believer departs for eternal glory (Ephesians 1:6). We believers are only sinners who have been "justified freely" by our Savior Jesus Christ (Romans 3:23,24). We deserve death, but God gives us "eternal life in Christ Jesus our

Lord" (Romans 6:23). Scripture does not praise us, "for it is *by grace you have been saved*, through faith—and this not from yourselves, it is the gift of God—not by works, so that no one can boast" (Ephesians 2:8,9). Our pastors seek to follow God's Word, which says, "If anyone speaks, he should do it as one speaking the very words of God . . . , *so that in all things God may be praised through Jesus Christ. To him be the glory and the power for ever and ever. Amen*" (1 Peter 4:11).

Why is the casket usually closed before the funeral service?

First of all, not all have the same customs. The casket is not always closed during funeral services, but it might be commonly done. It is certainly a very helpful custom to close the casket before a funeral service because it encourages people to focus their attention on God's Word, instead of on the body of the departed.

Remember what is and isn't the purpose of a funeral service. A Christian funeral is a worship service, conducted in the name of the triune God. It focuses attention on God's Word. It praises God. It offers gospel comfort to those who mourn. It is much less distracting to have the family members pay their last respects and to close the casket before the worship service begins.

Occasionally, pastors experience disappointment in some funeral customs. After his message from God's Word has focused hearts on the Savior and his Word, why would we want to focus attention on the body of the deceased by looking again at the lifeless body in an open casket? That body in the casket is not the person who died. That believer's soul is in heaven. It is good to leave the funeral service focused on the comforting promises of our gracious and loving Savior, instead of evoking the strong emotions of sadness when viewing the lifeless body yet one more time.

Though the departed loved one is gone, Jesus and his Word are present in the service (Matthew 18:20). It is best if our attention is riveted on the comforting words of our gracious God (Romans 10:17; Luke 10:38-42).

When considering funeral customs, it is good to keep in mind two Bible passages. Ecclesiastes 5:1 says, "Guard your steps when you go to the house of God. Go near *to listen* rather than to offer the sacrifice of fools, who do not know that they do wrong." Our purpose is to listen and to praise God. Genesis 28:17 simply records the awe that we should have in God's house, where his saving Word is proclaimed: "How awesome is this place! This is none other than *the house of God;* this is the gate of heaven." With that in mind, may we conduct ourselves with fitting reverence.

Why do we have Christian burials?

The Bible does not explicitly command us to conduct Christian burials. Certainly, many believers have done this in the past. Consider the patriarchs.

> I am about to be gathered to my people. Bury me with my fathers in the cave . . . in the field of Machpelah, near Mamre in Canaan, which Abraham bought as a burial place from Ephron the Hittite, along with the field. There Abraham and his wife Sarah were buried, there Isaac and his wife Rebekah were buried, and there I buried Leah." (Genesis 49:29-31)

The reason why Jacob wanted to be buried with them had everything to do with his faith. "For he was looking forward to the city with foundations, whose architect and builder is God" (Hebrews 11:10). He confessed that when he died, he would find "rest" with his believing ancestors (Genesis 47:30). Luther wrote:

> On the basis of these testimonies of Scripture the fathers concluded that there is another life and that the saints do not die and perish like brutes but are gathered to the people in the land of the living. Undoubtedly this fact, their certain expectation of another life, is the reason why they were so reverently and honorably buried by their children.[50]

The New Testament tells us about the burial of our Savior. "Joseph took the body, wrapped it in a clean linen cloth, and placed it in his own new tomb that he had cut out of the rock. He rolled a big stone in front of the entrance to the tomb and went away" (Matthew 27:59,60). John reveals that this "was in accordance with Jewish burial customs" (John 19:40). Of course, Jesus would rise from death and come out of that tomb on the third day.

In the book of Acts, we read that "godly men buried Stephen and mourned deeply for him" (Acts 8:2). Certainly we can sense respect in the burial customs. Yet there is more. The men who buried Stephen were godly and confessed the same faith that Stephen died confessing.

Some people in Bible times did not have honorable burials. Wicked Queen Jezebel is one example. The dogs devoured her body so that she was not buried; her body was "like refuse on the ground" (2 Kings 9:10,36,37). The Lord said that Jehoiakim would have "the burial of a donkey—dragged away and thrown outside the gates of Jerusalem" (Jeremiah 22:19). This was a sign of God's disfavor on his enemies. Ecclesiastes 6:3 describes the impact of not having a proper burial: "A man may have a hundred children and live many years; yet no matter how long he lives, if he cannot enjoy his prosperity and does not receive proper burial, I say that a stillborn child is better off than he."

In a Christian burial, we are confessing our faith that "all who are in their graves will hear his voice and come out" and that believers "will rise to live" (John 5:28,29). We are essentially saying what believing Martha said long ago: "I know he will rise again in the resurrection at the last day" (11:24). When the resurrection chapter of the Bible (1 Corinthians 15) talks about the body being "sown," or planted, it is describing burial. When it mentions that the body is "raised" it is reminding us of the "resurrection of the dead" on the Last Day (verses 42-44). There is a picture there of planting a seed with a harvest to follow. We will rise and come out of the grave, just as our Savior did on Easter Sunday.

Is it wrong to be cremated?

Cremation is not specifically commanded or forbidden in Scripture. It falls into the category of adiaphora (middle things; things neither commanded nor forbidden by God). So, the decision about cremation is a matter of Christian judgment.

Though burial was the standard practice among believers, there are a couple of examples of cremation in Scripture. After Achan and his family were stoned, their bodies were "burned" (Joshua 7:25). The bodies of Saul and his sons were "burned" (1 Samuel 31:11,12).

Some bodies are cremated to stop the spread of disease, to transport the remains more easily, and because it is less expensive. Unbelievers have had their bodies cremated and their ashes spread across the ocean in an attempt to escape from final judgment. They will not succeed. Those people will appear bodily before Jesus on judgment day.

This last reason for cremation has become more common in the past few decades. This has led many believers to look with disfavor on cremation. Some believers feel that it shows disrespect for the body God created. Some fear that they will be viewed as one of those unbelievers trying to escape the final judgment. And some just find the idea of receiving someone's ashes in a can unthinkable or repulsive.

Whatever your opinion happens to be, we must restate that Scripture neither commands nor forbids cremation. While I see no reason to encourage cremation, I know that our Lord is fully capable of raising ashes to life. We say in the common burial rite, "earth to earth, ashes to ashes, dust to dust," yet on the Last Day, the body will be raised. "For we must all appear before the judgment seat of Christ, that each one may receive what is due him for the things done while in the body, whether good or bad" (2 Corinthians 5:10). As long as someone is not trying to avoid the final judgment, we must regard cremation as a matter of Christian freedom.

Do the spirits of the departed remain here with us or haunt houses?

Remember what Scripture says about the spirits of people who have died. "The dust returns to the ground it came from, and the spirit returns to God who gave it" (Ecclesiastes 12:7). The souls, or spirits, of the departed do not hover around us. They depart from this life. God sends them to heaven or to hell. "Man is destined to die once, and after that to face judgment" (Hebrews 9:27).

There are many who ask about ghosts and haunted houses. Some Christians say that they have seen ghosts in their homes. In some cases, the sounds in so-called haunted houses might have physical explanations. Sometimes, old houses with creaky doors and floors may make spooky sounds that are hard to explain. Some houses probably are haunted.

I have occasionally surprised members of our congregation who are new to Bible class when I clearly declare that there are ghosts. I have absolutely no doubt that there are ghosts. But these ghosts are not the spirits (or souls) of people who have died. The ghosts I'm talking about are evil spirits or demons. Scripture plainly teaches that there are demons. They are evil angels who fell away with the devil. They are condemned to hell.

Somehow, they have possessed people. We often read of Jesus casting out demons. Matthew 8:16 says, "Many who were demon-possessed were brought to him, and he drove out the spirits with a word." This reminds us that our Lord and Savior has ultimate power over the demons. People noticed this and said of Jesus, "He even gives orders to evil spirits and they obey him" (Mark 1:27). These, not the spirits of the departed, are the ghosts that I say exist.

These ghosts (who are usually called demons, evil angels, evil spirits) have the capability of knowing things that people would not know and can imitate the appearance and sound of the departed. They can look like and sound like a departed loved one. They can even know the secrets of the departed. Over the years, people have mentioned that Houdini had some secret that he shared only with his wife. The demons could easily know that secret and pretend to be Houdini. These evil angels are capable of haunting houses as "ghosts."

These ghosts are not to be trifled with. Acts 19:11-16 teaches this very clearly by relating a true story.

> God did extraordinary miracles through Paul, so that even handkerchiefs and aprons that had touched him were taken to the sick, and their illnesses were cured and the evil spirits left them.

> Some Jews who went around driving out evil spirits tried to invoke the name of the Lord Jesus over those who were demon-possessed. They would say, "In the name of Jesus, whom Paul preaches, I command you to come out." Seven sons of Sceva, a Jewish chief priest, were doing this. One day the evil spirit answered them, "Jesus I know, and I know about Paul, but who are you?" Then the man who had the evil spirit jumped on them and overpowered them all. He gave them such a beating that they ran out of the house naked and bleeding.

Those who have heard about *The Exorcist*, in movie or book form, certainly get the point that evil spirits are not to be the objects of play. They can possess people. And they can possess places. Playing an occult game, such as using a Ouija board, involves inviting the evil spirits in. Once invited, these demons are not likely to leave. This is how some houses have become haunted. Siegbert Becker wrote:

> Closely related to the demoniac possession of persons is the possession of places. Stories of haunted houses are common in America but even more common in Europe. I suppose that all of us are inclined to write off such stories as the pure products of an overactive imagination. While we surely ought to be on our guard against naive credulity, yet the conclusions of trained observers would seem to indicate that some of these accounts are based on actual occurrences that defy a natural explanation. Parapsycholo-

gists usually speak of such "hauntings" as "poltergeist phenomena." . . . Many of these phenomena are associated
with spiritism and devil possession. . . . In Christian coun-
tries the houses are exorcised and the spirits are commanded to leave in Jesus' name.[51]

Are the departed souls of believers aware of us and earthly events?

Many false ideas have been disseminated through
movies and television shows. The movie *Ghost* depicts a
man who has died but whose soul stayed around earth to
influence events. Other movies and shows make it seem
like departed loved ones are either living in our houses or
at least looking down on us. This false idea does not come
from God's Word.

Isaiah 63:16 reveals that God is aware of us "though
Abraham does not know us or Israel acknowledge us."
Abraham is in heaven but is not aware of us. Israel is in
heaven but does not answer. In the People's Bible commentary, John Braun commented on this passage: "Once
believers die, they know the joys of heaven, but they do
not know the affairs of the loved ones they leave behind."[52]
Luther, who was certainly familiar with the Roman
Catholic practice of praying to departed saints, wrote:

> Those people are dead and know nothing of us. Here the
> scholastic doctors argue a great deal and come to various
> conclusions about how the fathers help and concern
> themselves with our affairs, and one renounces the other.
> But here the Holy Spirit teaches that the saints are dead,
> certainly they are dead to us. . . . Certainly God is the
> God of the living and the dead, but the saints are dead to
> us. Therefore the dead . . . should no longer be invoked,
> since they are not concerned about our affairs.[53]

We should not pray to the dead. We should not pray to Mary or the saints. They do not hear us. They cannot help us. We should not consult them for help or answers. When people claim to receive word from beyond the grave, they are likely hearing from the network of evil spirits. These evil angels know many secrets since they have been listening closely. They also have access to all those who have been condemned. We should steer far away from spirit mediums: "When men tell you to consult mediums and spiritists, who whisper and mutter, should not a people inquire of their God? Why consult the dead on behalf of the living? To the law and to the testimony! If they do not speak according to this word, they have no light of dawn" (Isaiah 8:19,20).

Hezekiah was right when he spoke of his life after death: "No longer will I look on mankind, or be with those who now dwell in this world" (Isaiah 38:11). Those who die in faith are in heaven. Those who die in unbelief are in hell. The souls of the departed are no longer with us.

Will I know my believing loved ones in heaven?

This is a very common question. Since the disciples easily recognized Moses and Elijah in the account of Christ's transfiguration, I see no reason why we wouldn't be able to know our fellow believers in heaven (Matthew 17:3,4). In Matthew 8:11, Jesus reveals that "many will come from the east and the west, and will take their places at the feast with Abraham, Isaac and Jacob in the kingdom of heaven." We know that we will be with the other believers. Would they be strangers to us? It hardly seems likely that we would spend eternity in heaven without knowing our fellow believers. Also, the apostle Paul said that the believers of Thessalonica would be his glory and joy on judgment day. This presumes that Paul would recognize them. Paul wrote, "What is our hope, our joy, or the crown in which we will glory in the presence of our Lord Jesus when he comes? Is it not you? Indeed, you are our glory and joy" (1 Thessalonians 2:19,20).

We sometimes speak of a "happy reunion in heaven." We mean this in the sense of Hebrews 12:22,23, which describes the heavenly Jerusalem as a joyful assembly: "You have come to Mount Zion, to the heavenly Jerusalem, the city of the living God. You have come to thousands upon thousands of angels in *joyful assembly*, to the church of the firstborn, whose names are written in heaven. You have come to God, the judge of all men, to the spirits of righteous men made perfect."

We will be assembled together with our Savior, our fellow believers, and the holy angels in heaven. We will certainly recognize Jesus, just as the disciples did when he rose from death (Luke 24:31; John 20:20; 21:12). Why would we not recognize our fellow believers?

We probably should make a distinction between *heaven before* and *heaven after* judgment day. Before judgment day, the souls of the believers are in heaven. After judgment day, the believers will have glorified bodies (reunited with their souls). We do not have a specific Bible passage that tells us exactly what we will see in heaven, but it seems likely that we will recognize our fellow believers' bodies (Luke 24:39,40). If God could permit the apostle John to see the souls of departed martyrs, he can certainly make it possible for us to see and recognize the souls of our fellow believers there (Revelation 20:4).

Like believing Job, we will be most interested in seeing our Redeemer (Job 19:25-27). Yet Scripture also mentions our fellow believers. We will be "together with them" and "with the Lord forever" (1 Thessalonians 4:17).

Perhaps a word of caution is in order, though. Jesus does tell us that "when the dead rise, they will neither marry nor be given in marriage; they will be like the angels in heaven" (Mark 12:25). These words lead us to be cautious about describing heaven in worldly terms. Marriage will not continue in heaven. Marriage is a wonderful blessing from God for this life, but marriage will not continue in heaven. This is one reason why a widow or widower is free to remarry (Romans 7:2,3; 1 Corinthians 7:39).

Does a soul in heaven experience time?
Is eternity timelessness or endless time?

Occasionally, otherwise very fine theologians have said more than Scripture actually says in answering these questions. Some have insisted that eternity is timelessness. But when they based it on Revelation 10:6, they fell into trouble. That passage does not mean that there is no more time (timelessness), but that "there will be no more delay" before the end of the world. Judgment day would come without delay.

One passage seems to indicate that there might be a perception of time on the part of the souls in heaven. Revelation 6:10 says, "They called out in a loud voice, 'How long, Sovereign Lord, holy and true, until you judge the inhabitants of the earth and avenge our blood?'" These souls in heaven were apparently aware of the passage of some time and were eager to have God do his just work. They asked how long before he would avenge them. Siegbert Becker commented on this verse of Scripture:

The time evidently appears to be long to the souls of the martyrs. Many orthodox Lutheran commentators have been of the opinion that after death souls are not conscious of the passage of time. They define eternity as the absence of time, or timelessness. While the Bible makes it clear that eternity as an attribute of God is timelessness, it never indicates that the word eternity has the same meaning when it is applied to creatures. Time is a creation of God, and God therefore exists outside of and beyond time. It is also clear from Scripture that there is a tremendous difference between God's eternity and ours. His eternity has no beginning, but our eternal life has a beginning. It is thus certainly possible that while God's eternity is timelessness, our eternity is endless time, and because of that, even the souls in heaven are conscious of the passage of time, as seems to be the case here. However, we must be careful not to become too dogmatic on this point.[54]

Once again, I will side with Dr. Becker and refrain from saying more than Scripture clearly reveals. We will know the answer when we get to heaven.

How old will we seem to be when we rise from the dead?
Again, the best answer is that we will know for sure when we get there. Scripture has not plainly answered this question. Will babies become the adults they would have become on earth had they lived? Are the elderly returned to middle age or youth? We really don't know.

Some have said that we will all be youths, because that is the prime of life. But Jesus did not turn into a boy when he rose from the dead. Scripture says that he will "transform our lowly bodies so that they will be *like his glorious body*" (Philippians 3:21). Some pointed to this Bible passage as the basis for saying that we will be the age Jesus was when he rose from death. But "like" him means glorious and sinless. It might not refer to appearance of age (young or old).

Some say that we will appear to be the age we were when we died, without the effects of sin. They think that we will look the age we were at death (without the aches, pains, wrinkles, deformity, and other ill effects of aging). We don't know for sure. The book of Revelation might sound that way when it talks about the dead "both small and great" (11:18; 19:5).

I think that the closest Scripture comes to an answer might be in that familiar account of our Savior's transfiguration when it says that "there appeared before them Moses and Elijah" (Matthew 17:3). Elijah never died, but Moses must be placed in the category of the risen in this episode. That he was recognizable as a man, and not a young boy, seems to convey the idea that we will not all become youths.

We should not stretch the Scriptures to say more than they do. Even though our bodies will be like our Savior's, we must make a clear distinction. He is the God-man, and we aren't. His body had the marks or wounds even after his resurrection. These wounds helped the disciples identify him. These marks gave him glory by reminding the disciples of Christ's redeeming death. These wounds might be an exception to the rule that such wounds would disappear when our bodies are glorified. In a similar way, the martyrs might have some mark that indicates their martyrdom. In a vision of heaven, John was able to recognize beheaded martyrs (Revelation 20:4). We leave the matter up to God, whose will is always best. We simply do not yet know the answer to this question.

Might there be animals in heaven?

Yes, there very well might be animals in heaven after judgment day. Romans 8:21 reveals that "the creation itself will be liberated from its bondage to decay and brought into the glorious freedom of the children of God." The creation would seem to include animals, which would be released from this sinful world. When God first created this world and everything was perfect and sinless, there were animals. We are told that there will be a new heaven and a new earth. If we picture that as a return to the Garden of Eden perfection, there is no reason to assume that there could not be animals. The words in the creation account lead one to picture the new heaven and new earth with animals:

> God said, "Let the water teem with living creatures, and let birds fly above the earth across the expanse of the sky." So God created the great creatures of the sea and every living and moving thing with which the water teems, according to their kinds, and every winged bird according to its kind. And God saw that it was good. . . .
>
> And God said, "Let the land produce living creatures according to their kinds: livestock, creatures that move along the ground, and wild animals, each according to its kind." And it was so. God made the wild animals according to their kinds, the livestock according to their kinds, and all the creatures that move along the ground according to their kinds. And God saw that it was good. (Genesis 1:20-25)

It was good then to have animals as part of God's perfect creation. Everything will be good in the future too. That could mean that there will be animals in the new heaven and new earth. But we must wait to learn for sure what it will really be like.

What will we do in heaven?

We would like to know. Will we work? Will it be one long worship service? We should not picture heaven as one long, really boring worship service. While worship should not ever be boring to us, sometimes children think of heaven as a very, very long church service. That is perhaps not the best picture to have in the minds of our children. Yes, we will certainly praise God in heaven. That is one of the most common descriptions of heaven. And we will sing! Revelation 5:9 says, "They sang a new song: 'You are worthy to take the scroll and to open its seals, because you were slain, and with your blood you purchased men for God from every tribe and language and people and nation.'" (See also Revelation 14:3 and 15:3.) The new song praises God for saving people. When they say, "You are worthy," that is worship. We too will praise God for saving us! Our singing and worship will be pure joy in the presence of our Savior God. Our voices will be perfect. The Bible describes the use of a harp to accompany the singing. The music and songs and worship will be perfect. We can't even imagine how great it will be. People who may not sing very well here will sing perfectly there. Worship will never be boring in heaven.

Still, it is possible that we will also work in heaven, as Adam and Eve did before the fall into sin. Genesis 2:15 tells us that "The LORD God took the man and put him in the Garden of Eden to work it and take care of it." This work was not painful or tiresome. God's holy people would not become weary or sick of it. Work was a joy in the perfect world, before the fall into sin.

It seems likely that the new heaven and new earth will be similar to the Garden of Eden. It is possible that our life there could include joyful occupation with various activities. (See Luke 19:17,19.) The book of Revelation in several places says that we will "reign" with Jesus (3:21; 5:10; 22:5). We don't know exactly what this means. Perhaps we will have useful work in overseeing some aspect of the new heaven and new earth. Above all we know that God's will is going to be done in heaven (Matthew 6:10).

We know that we will see our Savior and worship him joyfully. But worship is more than just a formal service. Even now, we worship our Savior by the way that we serve him each and every day. Romans 12:1 says, "I urge you, brothers, in view of God's mercy, to offer your bodies as living sacrifices, holy and pleasing to God—this is your spiritual act of worship." Worship God by the way that you live and serve each day: at home, at work, and at play. Second Corinthians 5:15 says that Jesus "died for all, that those who live should no longer live for themselves but for him who died for them and was raised again." It could be that the worship in heaven will be partly formal worship and partly informal, in the way that we serve God in various God-pleasing activities (whatever those might be). We know that we will glorify God:

> Then a voice came from the throne, saying: "Praise our God, all you his servants, you who fear him, both small and great!"
>
> Then I heard what sounded like a great multitude, like the roar of rushing waters and like loud peals of thunder, shouting: "Hallelujah! For our Lord God Almighty reigns. Let us rejoice and be glad and give him glory!" (Revelation 19:5-7)

How can I reach out to those who don't believe?

This is a very important question. If you would like more help, please ask your pastor. He will be very happy to help you. The most important thing to remember is that God works faith through the gospel (Romans 10:17). The gospel (or good news) that Jesus came to save us all is the most important message in reaching out. Usually we will want to begin with the law, to show people their sins and their need for a Savior. Sometimes people already feel the effects of the law. They feel terribly guilty and are afraid to die. These people need to hear the gospel right away.

I think that the easiest way to reach out to someone is to share with them these words of John 3:16: "God so loved the world that he gave his one and only Son, that whoever believes in him shall not perish but have eternal life." God loved the whole wide world and everyone in it so much that he gave his only-begotten Son to be our Savior. Jesus was born that first Christmas as true God and true man in one person. Jesus grew up, living a perfect life. He had to do this, as our substitute, to redeem us. He had to live a completely sin-free life. Then, he had to receive the full punishment of the sins of the whole world. He endured this at the cross, where he suffered and died paying the wages of our sins (death). There, the Lamb of God took away the sin of the world. There, Jesus became "the atoning sacrifice for our sins, and not only for ours but also for the sins of the whole world" (1 John 2:2). Because he had paid our ransom price in full, and because God accepted that payment, Jesus rose from death. He had won the victory over sin, death, and the devil. Jesus rose from death because he had won forgiveness for you, me, and all the world. Now, we can say to anyone, "Jesus died on the cross for you and took all of your sins away." We can say, "You are forgiven through Christ." That is the gospel, the good news of salvation. Jesus says in John 3:16, "whoever believes in him shall not perish but have eternal life."

Believe in the Lord Jesus, and you will be saved in the final judgment! He saved you!

Jesus has given us the good news to proclaim to others. In fact, our Savior wants this message proclaimed to all the world. He says, "Go into all the world and preach the good news to all creation. Whoever believes and is baptized will be saved, but whoever does not believe will be condemned" (Mark 16:15,16).

Those who believe will enjoy heaven forever. Those who do not believe will suffer in hell forever. Whether or not we do mission work really matters, doesn't it? Let's be sure to reach out to as many people as possible for as long as the Lord leaves us on this earth. Then, we will be able to enjoy the perfect world God has prepared for his believers in heaven.

> God loved the world so that he gave
> His only Son the lost to save
> That all who would in him believe
> Should everlasting life receive.
>
> Be of good cheer, for God's own Son
> Forgives the sins that you have done.
> You're justified by Jesus' blood;
> Baptized, you are a child of God.
>
> When you are sick, when death draws near,
> This truth your troubled heart can cheer:
> Christ Jesus saves my soul from death—
> This is the anchor of my faith!
>
> Glory to God the Father, Son,
> And Holy Spirit, Three in One!
> To you, O blessed Trinity,
> Be praise now and eternally! (CW 391:1,4-6)

Endnotes

[1]Maurice S. Rawlings, M.D., *Before Death Comes* (Nashville: Thomas Nelson Publishers, 1980), pp. 44,45.

[2]Siegbert W. Becker, "Heaven and Hell," in *Our Great Heritage*, Vol. 3 (Milwaukee: Northwestern Publishing House, 1991), p. 675.

[3]Becker, "Heaven and Hell," p. 672.

[4]*Catechism of the Catholic Church* (New York: Catholic Book Publishing, 1994), pp. 268,269.

[5]Francis J. Ripley, *This Is the Faith* (Rockford, Illinois: Tan Books and Publishers, 2002), p. 395.

[6]Ripley, *This Is the Faith*, p. 62.

[7]Ripley, *This Is the Faith*, p. 407.

[8]Ripley, *This Is the Faith*, p. 407.

[9]*Catechism of the Catholic Church*, p. 269.

[10]Smalcald Articles, Part III, Article III, *The Book of Concord: The Confessions of the Evangelical Lutheran Church*, translated and edited by Theodore G. Tappert (Philadelphia: Fortress Press, 1959), p. 306.

[11]*This We Believe: A Statement of Belief of the Wisconsin Evangelical Lutheran Synod* (Milwaukee: Northwestern Publishing House, 1999), p. 36.

[12]*This We Believe*, p. 17.

[13]*Quest for the Unknown: Life Beyond Death* (Pleasantville, New York: Reader's Digest Association, 1992), p. 21.

[14]Maurice S. Rawlings, M.D., *Beyond Death's Door* (Nashville: Thomas Nelson Publishers, 1978), p. 45.

[15]Raymond A. Moody Jr., M.D., *Life after Life* (New York: Bantam Books, 1975), pp. 21-23.

[16]Raymond A. Moody Jr., M.D., *Reflections on Life after Life* (New York: Bantam Books, 1977), p. 36.

[17]Rawlings, *Beyond Death's Door*, p.11.

[18]Rawlings, *Beyond Death's Door*, pp. 24,25.

[19]Rawlings, *Beyond Death's Door*, pp. 17-19.

[20]Rawlings, *Beyond Death's Door*, pp. 20,21.

[21]Rawlings, *Beyond Death's Door*, pp. 62,63.

[22]Rawlings, *Beyond Death's Door*, p. 110.

[23]Rawlings, *Beyond Death's Door*, p. 27.

[24]Rawlings, *Beyond Death's Door*, p. 14.

[25]*Quest for the Unknown*, p. 26.

[26]Rawlings, *Beyond Death's Door*, p. 61.

[27]*Quest for the Unknown*, p. 29.

[28]*Quest for the Unknown*, p. 32.

[29]Siegbert W. Becker, *Wizards That Peep* (Milwaukee: Northwestern Publishing House, 1978), p. 5.

[30]*Quest for the Unknown*, p. 29.

[31]*Quest for the Unknown*, p. 21.

[32]*Quest for the Unknown*, p. 29.

[33]Rawlings, *Beyond Death's Door*, p. 75.

[34]*Quest for the Unknown*, p. 20.

[35]Siegbert W. Becker, *Revelation: The Distant Triumph Song* (Milwaukee: Northwestern Publishing House, 1985), p. 324.

[36]Dante Alighieri, *The Divine Comedy of Dante Alighieri*, translated by Charles Eliot Norton (Chicago: Encyclopaedia Britannica, 1952), p. 4.

[37]J. Schoneberg Setzer, *What's Left to Believe?* (Nashville: Abingdon, 1968), p.141, quoted in *Eschatological Prophecies and*

Current Misinterpretations by Wilbert R. Gawrisch (Milwaukee: Northwestern Publishing House, 1989), p. 90.

[38]Clark Pinnock, "Fire, Then Nothing," *Christianity Today*, March 20, 1987, p. 40, quoted in *Eschatological Prophecies*, Gawrisch, p. 89.

[39]Augsburg Confession, Article XVII, Tappert, p. 38.

[40]Setzer, *What's Left to Believe?* p.137, quoted in *Eschatological Prophecies*, Gawrisch, p. 90.

[41]Apology of the Augsburg Confession, Article XVII, Tappert, p. 224.

[42]Becker, "Heaven and Hell," p. 667.

[43]Becker, *Revelation*, p. 308.

[44]*This We Believe*, p. 35.

[45]Martin Luther, *Luther's Works*, edited by Jaroslav Pelikan and Helmut T. Lehmann, American Edition, Vol. 49 (St. Louis: Concordia Publishing House; Philadelphia: Fortress Press, 1955–1986), p. 323.

[46]*Luther's Works*, Vol. 28, p. 185.

[47]*Luther's Works*, Vol. 28, p. 173.

[48]Becker, "Heaven and Hell," p. 676.

[49]Herman W. Gockel, *Answer to Anxiety* (St. Louis: Concordia Publishing House, 1961), p. 38.

[50]Martin Luther, *What Luther Says: An Anthology*, compiled by Ewald M. Plass, Vol. 2 (St. Louis: Concordia Publishing House, 1959), p. 781.

[51]Becker, *Wizards That Peep*, pp. 94-96.

[52]John A. Braun, *Isaiah 40–66* of The People's Bible series (Milwaukee: Northwestern Publishing House, 2001), p. 362.

[53]*Luther's Works*, Vol. 17, p. 360.

[54]Becker, *Revelation*, p. 113.

For Further Reading

Becker, Siegbert W. "Heaven and Hell," reprinted in *Our Great Heritage*, Vol. 3, pp. 652-677. Milwaukee: Northwestern Publishing House, 1991.

Becker, Siegbert W. *Revelation: The Distant Triumph Song*. Milwaukee: Northwestern Publishing House, 1985.

Becker, Siegbert W. *Wizards That Peep*. Milwaukee: Northwestern Publishing House, 1978.

Brug, John F. "The Spiritual Body" (unpublished paper), Nov. 2, 1982, revised Sept. 21, 1987, available on the Wisconsin Lutheran Seminary Web site: www.wls.net.

Christian Life Resources (for more information and scriptural guidance on end-of-life issues): www.christianliferesources.com.

Gawrisch, Wilbert R. *Eschatological Prophecies and Current Misinterpretations*. Milwaukee: Northwestern Publishing House, 1989. Also found in *Wisconsin Lutheran Quarterly*, Vol. 84 (1987), pp. 125-140,201-216,278-297; and Vol. 85 (1988), pp. 109-126,197-219. Parts I, II, and V are also found in *Our Great Heritage*. Vol. 3, Ed. Lyle Lange. Milwaukee, Northwestern Publishing House, 1991. pp. 679-743.

Hoenecke, Adolf. *Evangelical Lutheran Dogmatics*, Vol. 4. Milwaukee: Northwestern Publishing House, 1999.

Mueller, John Theodore. *Christian Dogmatics*. St. Louis: Concordia Publishing House, 1955.

Pieper, Francis. *Christian Dogmatics*, Vol. 3. St. Louis: Concordia Publishing House, 1953.

Scripture Index

Subject Index